THE LAST IN

THE
LAST INTAKE

Mike Baker

TEMPLE

TEMPLE PUBLISHING COMPANY
London, England

First published in Great Britain 1995
by Temple Publishing Company
London, England

British Library Cataloguing-in-Publication Data.
A catalogue record for this book is available
from the British Library

ISBN 1 85977 090 8

Cover design by Harold King

All names in this story have been changed
so as not to embarrass anyone who recognises
himself, or any particular person(s) therein.

Printed & bound in England by
Antony Rowe Ltd, Chippenham, Wiltshire

*In Memory of my
Father, Jack and Grandfather, Tom*

Contents

Chapter One

Call up

BORN AT THE beginning of the Second World War in 1939, and not knowing that the world was in turmoil, I grew up in an environment where the Germans were the bad guys, and were the dreaded enemy. Also, I was innocent to the fact that I had a father who was away doing his bit for King and country. My mother used to tell me that one day my father would come home. Whoever he was!!

The person who took the place of my father in those early days was my grandfather, who was very militarily minded. During the First World War he was a sergeant in the Oxon and Bucks Regiment. He spent some of his time in the trenches at Ypres and the Somme. He, and many others were to become known as 'The Old Contemptibles'. Going by his Army photographs I could imagine him with his bushy moustache which he grew at the time, being a right disciplinarian with his men in the field. I wouldn't have liked to have been under his authority.

He was awarded the Military Medal for outstanding gallantry above and beyond the call of duty. I never did find out what it was that he did to be awarded this medal. I only enquired once from him, and that was when I was in my early teens.

He just said. 'I may have got the Military Medal my son, but the Officer who sent us out got the Military Cross, and he never even left the camp.'

The way he said it was as if he didn't approve of the officer, and held him in great contempt. So I never pushed the question any further. Even though he appeared an old man to me, he was an active member of Dad's Army (Home Guard). He was a small gentle man who between work and his duties in the Home Guard, tended his garden, and tried to provide his family with all the comforts that were available, which wasn't all that much as everything in those days was rationed. Sometimes these comforts came via the black market. Right to his dying day, I had the greatest respect and love for him, and even to this day miss him. Never did he at any time have to discipline me by having to raise a hand. He was without doubt the greatest influence on my life. I don't wish to take it away from my own father, but my grandfather was there during the days when my character was being moulded. In later years after the war, my father came into his own.

One of the pleasures during those early hot days, was watching aircraft, which occasionally flew over the rooftops of the houses. A few of them were big aircraft (Dakotas) taking off from a local civilian airfield, at Whitchurch (Bristol Airport), not more that a mile or two from my home. At the time, I didn't realise that it was also one of the secret airfields where the top brass and royalty sometimes used to fly to and from abroad.

It was years later that I found out that the aircraft that the film star, Leslie Howard was in, was *en route* from Lisbon to Bristol Airport, when it was shot down by the Germans. Because it was thought at the time that Winston Churchill, the then Prime Minister, was aboard.

Hence as a small boy, I couldn't understand why people were never allowed to go anywhere near the airfield, and told in no uncertain terms to go away by the guards who surrounded the airfield or, were patrolling down the local country lanes that led to the airfield. It was from this background that my first instincts to be interested in aircraft and the military started to appear. Although at the time I didn't understand it, but to a certain extent it was already in my blood due to my grandfather's background.

There was also another RAF airfield a few miles away at Lulsgate Bottom. This airfield was a training field for No 10 Elementary Flying Training School. The planes they used were Tiger Moths and Avro Ansons. RAF Lulsgate Bottom used Whitchurch airfield as an additional airfield for circuits and bumps. (Touching down and taking off straight away).

After the war had finished and years passed I started work at the age of fifteen, as a messenger boy for the General Post Office delivering telegrams. This was through the insistence of my father, who believed that the General Post Office was a more secure job because it was part of the civil service. I, on my part, wanted to work at the BAC (British Aircraft Company, formerly the Bristol Aeroplane Company) as an airframe fitter.

At eighteen years of age I was one of many thousands of lads who had to go through the experience of trying to become a man, or a mouse, at the expense of Her Majesty's Service. That experience was called National Service. In those days, one would leave the so-called easy life of school, and start work at the age of fifteen take up an apprenticeship, or work for some firm as a labourer for a pittance of a few shillings a week just to earn a crust of bread. Although in saying a 'pittance' a working wage for most married men in those days was only two or three pounds. This was the 1950s.

These were the days of the Teddy Boys, with their drainpipe trousers, velvet coats and DA (Duck's Ass) haircuts, etc. and Mods and Rockers with their motorcycles and scooters. All out to impress the local talent. (girls) Fights would sometimes break out between the three factions. The police sometimes had their hands full trying to keep the peace.

The lads would meet of an evening, or at work, questioning one another about when they were due to go into the Services, and which one they would like to go in; when would they be getting their medical, and how one could get out of doing National Service by having this or that wrong with one's health. They would be deaf, or have some venereal disease or other. For some, they used any excuse to get out of doing their little bit. Many weird and wonderful stories came about on how to get out of doing National Service. It was, for many, an experience that just wasn't wanted.

The thought of having to have their hair cut to a short back and sides was an absolute insult to their dignity, and it was just not on.

'No bastard's going to cut my DA and spoil my hair. If they do then they're in for trouble and will have to answer to me,' was one of the comments. And they meant every word of these threats. What a surprise was in store for them. Even I didn't know what to expect from National Service; what Service I was to go in, or what I wanted to go in. We had heard so many harrowing stories of what went on from friends who were home on leave. It just didn't seem possible that men could be so degraded, and the insults one could receive from the NCOs and officers. This left an air of great apprehension as to what was to become of us once we were in the hands of these Service bully boys. For some – and I was one of these frightened lads – the stories that were coming out with really did frighten the living day lights out of us.

We were also at the period of time, when the government were to disband National Service, and make the military a voluntary force of professionals. So some of the lads that were due to go in to do their little bit were hoping, or telling themselves, that they may not have to go in after all. My father and I discussed the probabilities of my having to go in. What Service should I go for. My father and grandfather enlightened me on both their experiences of the Forces. My father having been in the North African, Italian campaign, and my grandfather in Europe during the wars said that I should try to get into the Royal Air Force. I asked why? My father's comment came as quite a surprise, especially as he was an Army man like my grandfather.

'You go in the Royal Air Force my son as they look after their personnel, even in the time of war. The Army and Navy don't so much.'

That was all the advice that I required. My grandfather stated much the same opinion. So it was to be the Royal Air Force for me. The only trouble was, as National Service was being run down the Royal Air Force were not taking on so many National Servicemen. I was now twenty years of age, going on twenty-one, and I still hadn't had my call-up papers. I was beginning to think that I was not going to go in and was quietly getting jubilant, that I was out of it. It was common knowledge that the month of my birth was possibly going to be the last intake of National Servicemen. Some would be taken in and some would not be required.

One morning, my mother called out to me to get up as there was a letter for me marked OHMS. I thought it was probably the Inland Revenue asking some more questions on my earnings so I opened the letter quite casually wondering, what in the hell do they want from me now? I fell silent for a moment. My mother asked what was wrong.

'I've got my call-up papers, I said, but under my breath, I was saying to myself, the bleeders have got me.

I was shaken to the core. How could they do this to me. Just as I'd got a girl and was going steady. I'm not bloody going. Balls to them, I thought.

My mother interrupted my thoughts. 'You got your call-up

papers?' she asked, sounding surprised. 'When have you got to go in?'
she enquired. 'Let me have a look at it,' she asked.

'It doesn't say when I've to go in Mum. It just says that I have to
report for a medical at Woodland Road later this month,' I replied.

As the time came closer for the big 'M' it was all I could talk about
with my mates at work and to my girlfriend. The lads were as usual,
asking what mob I was going to try for. So I said the RAF.

'You got no chance of getting into the RAF, or the Navy now.
You'll end up in the Army like the rest of us. That's where everyone's
ending up nowadays. The RAF and Navy are only taking regulars.'

This was the normal type of comment, or, 'No! you got it wrong.
They won't take you in the Air Force, unless it's the RAF Regiment.
Which is no more than the RAF's equivalent of the Army.'

These sorts of comments didn't exactly help my morale. All I
wanted now was to go in the RAF and nothing would distract me. It
was the Royal Air Force or nothing. My stomach was slowly getting
more knotted up as the medical came closer. What will I do if I don't
get into the RAF? I was gradually feeling more gutted. One day, I
would take on an attitude of nonchalance, couldn't care less. Another
day, I would be really uptight, and would be very quiet, and not say
much to anyone – which was not really my normal self. My girlfriend
didn't exactly help matters either, as she seemed to be more offhand
these days, and our relationship seemed to be cooling off.

The day of the medical came. I got up in the morning feeling as if
a great weight had been taken off my mind. I felt not exactly jubilant.
But my mind was clear, and I thought.

'Well, kid, your girl's ditched you, and you're now going into the
Services, regardless of what mob you're going into. So you got to do
it. Let's go in it and sod the lot of them. I'M GOING TO BLOODY
WELL ENJOY MYSELF.'

The Medical Centre when I arrived was full of lads that were there for
the same reason. Whilst we sat around waiting for our turn for documentation, medical checks, etc, we spoke about our chances and fears,
what mob we wanted to go in, and so on. The usual comments came
back at me when I mentioned going into the RAF.

'Fat chance of going into that lot mate. They're not taking National
Servicemen now.'

Eventually my name was called. At the table I went to, the usual questions were asked in the usual drawling, uninterested tone.

Name?
Address?
Date of Birth?
Occupation?
Religion?
Are your father and mother alive?

And so on and so on. Then the question that I had been waiting for.

'WHAT SERVICE DO YOU WISH TO ENTER?'

'Could I go in for the Royal Air Force please, sir,' in a very quiet and weak sort of manner, I said as if it was an insult to the questioner's dignity.

He looked at me from above his spectacles with a look of disbelief. Raising an eyebrow as much as to say, 'Fat chance you got of that, laddie.' His eyes went down to the paper in front of him, and he ticked off the necessary box.

'OK! That's all. If you would like to go into the other room over there and wait for the medical doctor,' he said, pointing so matter of factly. 'He'll see you in a moment.'

'Thank you,' I replied, very meekly, and proceeded into the next room.

This room was a typical government room, large, green painted walls, cold and quite abhorrent.

'Sit over there please sir.' I heard as I came through the door from the other room. I started to walk to the row of chairs that had been pointed out to me.

'And take off your clothes, except your underpants,' was said, as if in afterthought.

I proceeded to take off my clothes, along with the other lads, feeling very conspicuous, as if everyone was looking at me. After undressing as requested, I decided I was not exactly enjoying my first mass medical. I sat on the chair waiting for further instructions. I waited for a little while, slowly getting cold, and listening for announcements on my turn to go in.

'Next!' came the call. It was now my turn.

'In that room sonny' said the orderly. I meekly followed his instructions and went into the room as requested. Inside the room a doctor sat at a table with a pile of files on each side of him, with my file presumably in front. Standing to the side of him was a nurse going about her duties. She never even looked up as I came in.

'Alright son, there's nothing to worry about. This medical won't be any different from when you were at school,' he said.

At last! A friendly face, I thought. The doctor began to check my chest, eyesight, height, and so on.

'If you would like to drop your underpants,' he said in a rather fatherly tone. I dropped my underpants and stood there completely naked, feeling absolutely petrified. I had never had this done at school. I stood there as he took a spatula, and lifted one testicle and then the other. My god that spatula was cold!

'Cough,' he demanded. I coughed as requested, wondering what he wanted me to do that for.

'Again,' he ordered as he lifted up the other testicle. I was bloody glad my mother had demanded that I had a good bath before I left that morning . . .

'Right son, over there, behind the screen is a bottle. Would you fill it up a little and then bring it back please,' he requested. I proceeded over to the screen. Went behind it, found the small bottle and filled the bottle from the tap. I came back to the doctor, giving him the bottle as I approached him. He looked at it.

'No, no, no, my son. I don't want the water from the tap.' He said at the same time looking and nodding down at between my legs.

'Oh!' was all I could reply, feeling as embarrassed as could be. I'm sure my face was as red as a beetroot. Well, I couldn't help it. It was the first time I had had an experience like this. I was still quite innocent in the world. I returned behind the screen to give a sample of my urine. As if to read my mind the doctor called from his seat.

'Turn on the tap, my son, it might make it a little easier.'

I came back after a while feeling a right idiot. The nurse was still doing her duties at the side, but I'm sure she had a smirk on her face, which made me feel even more embarrassed.

'You can put your pants on again now my son.' said the doctor. 'Sit down here,' he pointed to the wooden chair, 'and cross your legs please.'

I sat as requested, not knowing what was going on now, and not knowing what was to become of me. I was now completely flustered.

I had never, ever had a medical like this before. What does he mean. This medical *won't* be any different from when you were at school, I thought I've never had a medical anything like this before. What's he going to do to me next.

The nurse gave the doctor a small hard rubber hammer. He proceeded to hit my kneecaps. My kneecap responded by nearly kicking him. 'Cross your other leg please,' he said. I did as I was told. He then knocked my other knee, again with the same result. The doctor said something to the nurse who then went out of the room. As she exited the doctor sat on the edge of his table and said, 'Well now! You're as fit as can be, my son. A1 in fact. Now, is there anything that you may be concerned about as regards your health?'

Now's my chance of getting out of it. My mind was saying to me.

'Well yes there is,' I started. 'When I was younger, I had pleurisy, which was very painful at the time. I find that since then I have always had trouble keeping my breath when running any distance.'

The quack looked at me and replied. 'I have checked your chest, back and front, and there's no trace of pleurisy there now. I don't think you need worry about that any more. Your chest is as clear as a bell.'

Well, that was that. I was in the Services, whether I liked it or not. Who cares anyway, I thought nonchalantly.

'If you would like to go back into the other room and get dressed and wait, I think the careers officer will want to see you next,' the doctor said in a matter of fact tone as I went back outside.

'Next!' was shouted out so the following unsuspecting individual could go in and be treated like an animal up for the slaughter.

I meanwhile got dressed along with a few other fellows.

'How did you get on?' One of the chaps next to me said as he was putting on his tie.

'Oh, I'm in it whether I like it or not. I'm A1' I replied.

'And me, worse luck.'

After getting dressed, we were ushered into a corridor. We were told to sit down on the chairs which were lining the walls and wait. As usual, the chairs were wooden and the corridor just as spartan as all the other rooms we had been through.

'My name's Mike,' I said to the other chap who had been dressing next to me.

'And I'm Pete. Pleased to meet you mate. Only wish we'd met in better circumstances,' he said.

It was really friendship for mutual comfort rather than a lasting friendship. Once we were out of this forbidding establishment I doubted if I would ever meet him again. The door which we sat next to had a sign pinned to it. It said 'Careers Officer.' Another civil servant opened the door from inside and poked his head round the door. He called a name. The man named was taken in. The rest of us had to wait until called.

Pete said to me, 'I hope to be going into the Navy if I can. My dad was in the Navy, so I got a pretty good chance of getting in.'

He said this to me with confidence, as if he had some inside information, and as if it was all fixed for him.

The door opened. The head came round the door again. 'Mr P Miller, please.'

'That's me,' said Pete. He jumped up and disappeared inside the door. After what seemed like ages the door opened, and my name was called. As I entered the room, which seemed a lot more hospitable, with the room being carpeted, and having cupboards around the walls. At the desk sat a gentleman with my file placed in front of him.

'Mr Baker?' he enquired.

'Yes,' I replied.

He asked if the address that he had was the one that I resided at. This I confirmed.

'I understand that you want to go into the Royal Air Force?' he asked. Before I could answer he went on, 'Why do you want to go into the Royal Air Force?

My mind was in a turmoil, and I hadn't expected the procedures that I was going through in this establishment.

'Well,' I said hesitantly. 'All my life I have been living near an airfield. I've been interested in aircraft. And I spend a lot of time at the local airfield watching civil aircraft come in and take off.' This was no lie, as if it had not been for my father I would have been in the aircraft business with an apprenticeship, after leaving school. For no reason at all, I then made the statement to the careers officer. 'If I like the life, I'm seriously thinking of signing up.' Why had I lied with that statement, for the rest of my life, I shall never know.

The Careers Officer asked me a few more questions but of no significance that I could see. Finishing the interview he pointed me to another door. I had wondered where the other lads had gone, as they never came out of the door that they went in.

'If you would like to sit in the lobby next door I will get a recruiting officer to interview you.' With that he opened the door for me to go out.

In the lobby were the fellows that had gone into see the Careers Officer before me, including Pete. I sat down beside him.

'How goes it?' I asked him.

'OK,' he replied confidently.

It seemed no sooner had I sat down, when my name was called out. I followed the attendant upstairs as requested, along what seemed like a long corridor, until he came to a door. He stopped. Knocked on the door and waited for the person inside to call out 'Come in.' I followed him in, not knowing what to expect.

Seated at a table was an RAF Officer. He said to the attendant. 'Thank you, Sims. Wait outside.' Turning to me. He stood up. Offered his hand in a handshake which I returned, not out of enthusiasm, but out of politeness.

'Mr Baker?' he asked. 'Pleased to meet you. Please take a seat.' I sat at the table, completely mesmerised by the uniform. 'I understand that you wish to join the Royal Air Force,' he stated.

'Yes!' I said, being jolted out of my stupor. 'Yes, that's right, sir,' I replied again more enthusisatically.

'Why do you want to join the Royal Air Force?' he asked.

'Because, I've always been interested in aircraft. Lived very near an airfield all my life,' and then added the comment, 'If I like the life, I am seriously thinking of signing up,' as I had said before.

'If you do get into the RAF, Mr Baker – and I'm not saying that you will,' he added quickly, 'would you want to go abroad?'

I had never thought of a question of this nature being put to me, so instinctively I replied, 'Oh yes, the further away from this country the better.'

'Why do you want to go abroad with the Royal Air Force then?' the officer asked.

I could sense that my answers had to be certain ones. I added, lying through my teeth, 'Well, I would like to see what life in the RAF is like abroad first before I sign on.' I then added, again lying through my teeth, 'After all, if I sign on, I shall sign on for the full whack of twenty-five years or whatever it is.'

'What hobbies do you have?' he then asked.

'Apart from watching aircraft, I have a motorcycle which I maintain.'

'You maintain your motorcycle?' he interrupted.

'Oh yes,' I acknowledged. 'I can strip a motorcycle right down to the main frame, and strip the engine and gearbox as well.'

'Where did you learn to do this then?' the recruiting officer asked.

'My father would not let me on to a motorcycle until I had learned to strip every part of it and then put it together again. Once I had done this my father said that I could go anywhere in the country. If anything went mechanically wrong I would have a pretty good chance of repairing it, and know how to go about it.'

'Your father is a very wise man,' he said. 'Talking about your father,' he went on. 'What was your father in? Army, Navy, or Royal Air Force?'

'My father was in the RASC. Backwards and forwards from the front line in an ambulance, picking up the wounded etc, through the North African and Italian campaigns,' I said.

'Your father saw quite a lot of action then,' he commented. I could see that the interview was coming to a close. 'Well thank you Mr Baker. If you would like to go downstairs again you will be notified which Service you are to be in later.' He stood up, and smiled, offering his hand in a handshake, wished me good-day, and I was out of the door. I went downstairs again into the main lobby, where all the others were sitting waiting to hear their fate. Amongst others, was Pete.

'How d'you get on? I asked, as I sat down beside him.

'No problem,' he replied. 'Piece of piss. Just got to wait for confirmation, that's all.'

'You saw the naval recruiting officer then?' I enquired.

'Yeah! As I said, no problem,' said Pete confidently. 'How about you?' he then asked me.

'Me? Well, I saw the RAF bloke, if that's what you mean. But I don't know whether I'm in or not. Probably the Army I expect,' I concluded.

'We'll know in a few minutes, one way or the other,' Pete broke in.

All the chaps in the lobby were talking to one another, more out of cold comfort than anything else, all wondering what the future held in store for them. Approximately half an hour went by before a civil servant came in. In his hand was a list.

'Gentlemen,' he began, 'if you will bear with me and listen for your names, I will be able to tell you what Service you have been selected for.'

The Lobby fell quiet, except for the nervous cough from one or two.

'Barnes C – Army,' he started.
'Harris B – Army.'
'Isaacs T – Army.'
'Bryant F – Army.'

He went on through the names. Most were destined for the Army, but a very few were destined for the RAF. As each name was called, there was either a sigh of relief, or a grunt.

'Miller. P – Army.'

'Bloody hell!' Pete said out loud. 'Are you sure you have the right bleeding person? I was down for the Navy.' he interrupted indignantly.

'Your name is Peter Miller?' the civil servant enquired of him.

'Yes, I'm Peter Miller.'

'And you're the only Peter Miller here aren't you?' the orderly asked, as he looked around for another possible Peter Miller. There was no reply.

'Army,' he retorted, giving the word 'Army' more emphasis.

Amongst the rest of the fellows there were a few sniggers. A few more names were called out. Then, 'Baker. M.'

My heart missed a beat as my name was called.

'RAF,' came the answer.

A sigh of relief.

'You did say RAF, didn't you sir,' I asked, not believing my luck.

'You heard me. RAF,' he repeated.

A smile of absolute joy must have come over my face, as the chap next to me leaned over to me and whispered, 'Stupid bugger. Not the RAF,' he whispered, 'it means the RAF Regiment you're in, mate.'

I couldn't have cared less. As far as I was concerned I wasn't in the Army, that was the all-important thing to me. The civil servant finished the list of names. Some were relieved that they now knew what Service they were going to serve in for the next two years. Some were absolutely devastated by the news. Pete was very quiet and bruised. His confidence was completely shattered.

'This will all be confirmed by post,' said the Civil Servant.

'You will also be informed at the same time what date, and where to report for National Service,' he concluded. 'That is all, gentlemen. You may leave.'

Chapter Two

The First Day

THROUGH THE LETTERBOX came the long awaited letter. My mother couldn't wait for me to open the letter, and read it out aloud for the rest of the family to hear.

'Dear Sir,
        You are hereby instructed to report on Wednesday 12th October to RAF Cardington by 18.00 hours. Enclosed is a rail warrant,' Etc. Etc.

Enclosed with the letter was an additional sheet of paper, that explained how I could get to RAF Cardington, via certain rail connections, also what articles of clothing to wear.

Well, that was it then. I was about to embark on something that was to change my whole life, although at the time I didn't appreciate it. I told my work-mates I was on my way shortly. I was still getting the odd wisecrack about it being the RAF Regiment, which lowered my morale a little. As I had been waiting so long for the letter to tell me to go I was now beginning to wonder whether it was to be the Regiment after all. It was now 1960, and quite a lot of my workmates, who were messengers boys with me had done their National Service and had already come out. I had now been waiting close on three years from the age of eighteen. I was no longer a messenger boy, but a postman.

On Tuesday, being my last day at work before going to Cardington, I happened to be working beside an older postman. George was his name. I imagined him to be in his late forties, early fifties. I mentioned to him that it was my last day at work for two years.

He said, 'Why, where are you off?'

'I'm going into the services for a couple of years,' I replied.

'Oh yeah, and what mob are you going into?' he enquired.

'Oh just the Air Force,' I stated in a casual manner.

'I was an RAF Officer, years ago,' he replied, in a more interested manner.

'What were you doing in the Air Force then George?'

'I was on the Air-Sea Rescue launches.' He paused then added, 'Out around Malta, during the war. Look!' George said before I could say anything else. 'For what it's worth, I'll give you some advice. You can take it or leave it. It's up to you.'

He took me by surprise. Here I was talking to an ex-RAF Officer, a man that had seen life in the RAF.

'What advice is this then, George?' I urged him.

'If you do just three things in the Services, you won't go far wrong.'

' Come on then. What are they?' I interrupted.

'If you do as you're told, don't answer back, and,' he said, using the word 'and' lingeringly, 'keep yourself reasonably tidy, you won't go far wrong,' He seemed to say the word 'reasonably' with emphasis.

'Thanks, George. I'll remember,' I said, not really taking it too seriously. I didn't realise at that time that this piece of advice would be so important to me, and so significant. I would come to remember those few words for the rest of my life.

Next day, I was up and out of bed reasonably early. I washed, dressed and was feeling quietly excited. I had to catch the early train for London Paddington station. From there, I was to go by underground to another station to catch the train for Bedford and at Bedford, I was to be picked up by bus and taken to Cardington.

My mother got me my favourite breakfast, which was a nice fried egg, bacon, sausage and beans. A typical English breakfast. She fussed over me like a broody hen. My father kept quiet, but I could see in his eyes that he was proud that his son was actually going into the services. My grandfather, which was most unusual for him, stayed in the background smoking his pipe, but his attitude towards me was different. I couldn't put my finger on it, but there was a difference. Most strange. I just couldn't make him out; I had never seen him like

this before. I often looked at him and all he would be doing was to be
staring at me with a smile on his face.

My father, accompanied by my mother and grandfather, took me
to the station in the family car. I got on the train, leaned out of the
door-window, and we talked about this and that, nothing of great
importance. My stomach was a little queasy, as I was embarking on
something unknown. Eventually the whistle went and the train was
ready to move off. We all said our goodbyes. As I shook hands with
my grandfather, he looked up and said. 'Don't worry my son. You'll
be alright.'

He must have sensed that I was very apprehensive about the whole
affair. 'Cheers Pop, and thanks,' I said as I shook his hand. With that,
the train was on its way to London. I was on my way to the great
unknown.

On arrival at Paddington station, I made my way to the
underground for the train to the other station, and from there, the
train for Bedford. During the whole train trip I felt lonely, yet excited.
Eventually I arrived at Bedford station, late in the afternoon. As I
came out of the station along with a couple of other lads who had got
off the same train, but from other carriages, I could see that there were
a couple of uniformed airmen talking to each other. They were
waiting just outside the station gates. They had peaked caps on, with
white tops. I approached them to ask the whereabouts of the bus for
Cardington. I spoke to the nearest one to me, who had his back to
me. 'Excuse me please,' I started. He turned around at the sound of
my voice. Without waiting, he said, 'Are you for RAF Cardington?'
before I could ask any more questions.

'Yes,' I replied.

It was then that I noticed that the two airmen had a red armband,
with black edges on their sleeve. Marked on their armband were the words
'RAF Police' printed in black in contrast to the background of red.

'Then get on that grey RAF coach over there,' he ordered. Then,
as if as an afterthought 'Please,' he said. I didn't argue with him, as
judging the way he ordered me onto the bus, he didn't sound as if he
was in a very good mood.

It was late afternoon, early evening, by the time the bus got to RAF
Cardington. One of the fellows who was on the bus mentioned that
Cardington was the airfield where the R101 and R102 Airships had
flown from and that the hangars there were the biggest in Britain. I

didn't know this, and wasn't really interested. It was all new to me, but I was more interested in what was going on outside. The bus stopped outside some buildings, after arriving through the gates of RAF Cardington. An Airman came onto the bus again – I think he was a policeman as well. He directed the driver to some other part of the camp. The bus finally stopped outside some wooden billets.

'Right lads, out you all get, this is the end of the journey.'

We all got out. 'Follow me!' he ordered. We followed him along the footpath, until we came to the billets we were to occupy.

'This will be your billet for the next few days, until you have all been fitted out with uniforms, etc,' he informed us. 'I want twelve of you to stay in this billet, and the rest of you go into the billet next door,' he ordered. 'You are not to move out of this billet until tomorrow when someone will come and pick you up in the morning.' With that, he took the rest of the guys to the next billet. The twelve of us that had been left selected a bed for the night. One of the new recruits looked up, and with a real Cockney accent, moaned, 'Miserable bugger! What does he mean, not to go out of the billet until the morning! Sod him. If I want to go out, then I'll go out.'

Another one of the lads who had selected a bed a couple of beds from me looked up and said, in a broad Scots accent, 'Well, I don't know about you lot. But I'm knackered. I've been up since three this morning. And I'm all for bed.'

As the lads in the billet sorted themselves out with their pyjamas, washing bags etc. Different comments came out about one thing or the other. There was a large cross-section of lads in the billet. Some had come from Scotland, some from the Midlands – in fact from all parts of the British Isles. Most of us were tired and just wanted to go to bed. As the lads were sorting themselves out, putting their personal belongings into the wooden lockers that were beside each bed, the uniformed Airman came back in again.

'Stand by your beds!' He ordered.

Everyone was more or less by their bed anyway. We all turned around towards the door that the Airman had just come through.

'I will be back in half an hour, to take you all to the mess for a meal,' he said. 'I expect some of you haven't eaten for a while.' With that he was gone.

'So much for your pit, Jock,' one of the lads said sarcastically. Everyone chuckled.

'What part of Scouse-land do you come from then, mate?' asked another of the inmates looking towards the chap who had cracked the joke at Jock's expense.

'Oh, I come from Merseyside, a place called Birkenhead,' he answered. Already a sort of comradeship was forming in the billet before we had unpacked. We were all in the same boat, so to speak, and needed each others' presence just for morale's sake. We were all in a strange place and a strange environment.

A half-hour later, we were taken to have a meal in the mess. Everything looked so strange and alien to us. We ate our meal, which on the whole wasn't too bad. Perhaps it was because most of us were etremely hungry. After the meal we were taken back to our billet as by now it was late, and we were all tired. It didn't take long for any of us to drop off even if some of us had a rather uneasy sleep because of the unfamiliar beds we were in.

'Good morning, Airmen. The time is now 06.00 hours. You have exactly one hour to get yourselves ready,' came the voice suddenly from the loudspeaker situated above the main door.

Some of the recruits stirred. Some just turned over and went back to sleep. Fifteen minutes later, the voice came again.

'Good morning Airmen. The time is now 06.15.' Everyone came to. Some not knowing where they were. Eventually everyone had got washed and dressed. Some were like zombies, some as bright as a bell, and some just followed quietly. I was one of the quiet ones. I felt alone, far from home, and was just not used to being woken up like this.

An Airman (in uniform) came into the billet at seven o'clock.

'Right lads,' he said. 'I will be your guide, for the next day or two.' He went on. 'You will be taken to the mess for breakfast, and then from there I will meet you all back here at 0800 hours, to tell you what's happening to you today.'

He led us off to the mess that we had been in the night before. When we arrived there seemed to be hundreds of new recruits, like us, still in civilian dress, having their breakfast. As we came in, they seemed to glance up sheepishly, wondering who was entering. After they realised the crowd coming in were no different to them, they went on with their breakfast, like sheep following one another. Everyone was in the same boat.

We got back to the billet a little after 0800 hours. The Airman was not very amused to be kept waiting.

'Today, you will be taken to the MO for a medical check-up,' he started. 'It won't be any different from the medical that you had when you were called up. If anything,' he added, 'it won't be so thorough as last time. Right! Line up outside on the road in lines of three,' he ordered.

We all did as instructed. I noticed for the first time that the Airman had two stripes on his sleeve, which made him a corporal. We were marched, if you can call it that, more like a stroll, to the MO's offices where we were then subjected to another medical as the Airman had said. It wasn't so severe as the earlier one that I had at Woodland Road thankfully. Once inside the MO's block we were lined up for a 'short' inspection in two rows. We were also ordered to drop our trousers so that we were naked from the waist down. A Medical Officer came in and proceeded to inspect our penises. He walked slowly in front of each one of us, with a stick or cane in his hand. As he passed each one of us he would lift our penis up, let go, then proceed to the next man. For the next day or two, we were marched around to several sections for one thing or the other. The day came that we were to be fitted out for our uniforms, and given our service number. We were marched to a hangar where there was a long table. 'Line up in single file,' we were ordered. We lined up and were then told to go down the line of tables, where we would be issued with our uniforms, underwear, knife and forks, and our housewife, by the Airmen behind the tables. Each item of clothing that we came to was more or less thrown at us, regardless whether it fitted or not.

'That's not my size,' one chap would say. 'Then swap it with one of your mates,' came back the reply. We were then instructed to line up in lines of three to go for our Service number. We were marched to another hangar with our uniforms under our arms or in our kit-bags, looking like a load of waifs and strays. In the next hangar stood another longish table. At the table sat three Airmen.

'Line up in single file,' we were instructed again. The first Airman had a large sheet of paper. On the paper was a list of numbers printed boldly. I noticed that the numbers started with 5081800 and went on up to 5082000. For once my mind seem to be in gear (something that it hadn't been for quite a few days).

'If I can get into the sixth position, I might be able to get the number that I want,' I told myself. This I did. I moved myself into the sixth position and waited for the line to move forward hoping that no one else would squeeze in front of me. My luck was in, we moved forward. The first recruit was given 5081800; the next 5081801; then the next three. Then it was my turn. My number was to be 5081805. It was a number that was the same frontwards as it was backwards. I couldn't forget that number could I? From that day onwards, I was to be 5081805 AC2 Baker. M. The lowest of the low – for a while at least. We were then marched back to our billet, where everyone tried on their uniforms. Some uniform trousers were too big, some too small. We swapped our uniforms, until we more or less had a comfortable uniform. The same went for our hats. Obviously a few were going to have uniforms that were unsuitable for them, but the unfortunate ones were to end up the fortunate ones. They were taken back to the uniform room, and completely fitted up with a uniform that was more or less made to measure for them.

From the next day on we were instructed to wear our uniforms all the time. Nevertheless although we were in uniform, none of us knew how to look smart in them. We were to learn very shortly, within twenty-four hours in fact, what Service discipline was all about. I had a rude awakening coming to me especially.

Our civilian clothing had to be wrapped up in parcels, addressed to our home address, then sent home courtesy of Her Majesty's Government. We were to be posted to RAF Bridgnorth, for what we were told would be for our Basic Training, whatever that meant. At 14.30 hours, we were to line up on the barrack square with our kit-bags. We were then to await further instructions. We had been told that a troop train was to take us to our new base in Shropshire, and that the railway station was over in the far corner of the airfield. From the barrack square to the station was a distance of approximately half a mile to three-quarters of a mile away.

At 14.30 hours an Officer came onto the square. He instructed us to answer 'Sir' when we heard our name, and the last four digits of the Service number, pick up our kit-bags, and march swiftly over to the station, where the train would be leaving at 17.00 hours. No one took too much notice of his instructions, other than that we were to go over to the station, once we heard our names called out.

'1866 Floyd. P' or some other such name and number was called out first.

'Yep!' was the answer.
'1832 Halifax. T'
'OK' was the reply, or something similar.
There was just no respect given to the Officer.
'1805 Baker, M.'
I replied 'Yes alright.'

I picked up my kit-bag and proceeded to walk over towards the station. I didn't hurry as there were plenty of Airmen still on the barrack square awaiting their names to be called out. I wandered over the airfield for about two hundred yards. I noticed in the distance a smallish man standing near the corner of the airfield. In fact, he looked like a midget due to the distance he was away from me. He brought his arm round in a swinging motion, so as to look at his wrist-watch. I heard a faint voice say very slowly, 'It's alright Airman. The train doesn't go for another three quarters of an hour at least.'

A little more clearly I heard him say. ' Take your tim-m-m-e,' and then as if the heavens had opened up the whole airfield could hear. A roar

'MOVE!'

Needless to say, I jumped. The bellow was intended for me. I moved a lot quicker towards him. I noticed the figure that had shouted at me unnecessarily − I thought − was a very small man who seemed to take great delight in shouting and bawling at me.

'Move yourself, Airman. You're in the Forces now!' he shouted at me again, as I came close to him. The small man who I noticed had RAF Regiment flashes on his shoulders, was also a Corporal. His peaked cap looked just as if it had come from the Guards. It had a short peak that came straight down his forehead. To look forward, he had to lift his head up; in fact just to be able to see. Around his waist he wore a white belt where his tunic buttons and brasses shone brightly. Tucked under his left arm was what looked like a cane.

'I'm your new father, my son, and unfortunately for you, I don't like lazy sods like you,' he screamed in my ear as I came up to him. As he shouted, I noticed that his eyes seemed to bulge out of their sockets, as if he took great delight in trying to belittle me.

'My name is Corporal Boon,' he screamed at me. 'By the time I've finished with you, I can promise, you'll wish you'd never known me. You won't forget Corporal Boon for the rest of your life. Stand still when I'm talking to you,' he bellowed at me, as I tried to walk past.

I stopped where I was not knowing what next.

'What's your name, Airman?' he asked.

I started 'AC,' But before I could say anymore. Corporal Boon interrupted me. 'I'll tell you when to speak Airman,' he bellowed again. 'You won't shave, sleep, or shit, unless I tell you from now on, Airman.'

'Bloody hell! What have I done to deserve this,' I thought.

'Now, what is your name again Airman?' the Corporal screamed, I hesitated, not knowing whether to speak or not.

'I asked you a question, Airman. Come on, come on. What's your name?' he screamed again. His face right opposite to mine, except he was looking slightly up at me. He seemed to be frothing at the mouth, and the eyes were bulging even more. 'Or have you bloody well forgotten your name already, Airman?'

'AC2 Baker,' I replied, frightened to say any more.

'Right AC2 Baker,' he shouted out mockingly. 'I shall be keeping an eye on you from now on Airman, I've taken a dislike to you already. So stay out of my way from now. You horrible little man you,' he finished.

By now I was shaking like hell. What in the hell have I let myself in for, I thought. Miserable bleeder.

'Now move it, move it, move it,' Corporal Boon started again, 'and get on that train.' Then he screamed as loud as he could, 'AT THE DOUBLE.'

I moved out of his way as fast as I could. Like he said, I had made an enemy, and I hadn't done anything to cause it, apart from walking over the airfield.

'Bloody hell, mate. What was that all about?' enquired one of the new recruits as we both got on the train. 'He's certainly got it in for you, ain't he.'

Chapter Three

RAF Bridgnorth

THE TRAIN LEFT RAF Cardington on time. It was dark and cloudy, due to the winter months closing in. No one knew anyone else as we had all been put on the train like cattle going to the slaughter house. Some of the recruits sat quietly. Some talked incenssantly to cover up their nerves. No one knew what to expect once we had arrived at Bridgnorth. I for one was very apprehensive, especially after my encounter with Corporal Boon. I tried to put him to the back of my mind, but could not. I had never been spoken to in such a manner, not even by my parents. Who in the hell was he to talk to me like that.

During the train journey I had cause to go to the toilet. My heart missed a beat, as I passed some NCOs. Amongst them was Corporal Boon. He had his cap off and I noticed that he had his hair cropped short, like the rest of the NCOs. As I passed him, our eyes crossed. I looked away quickly, as he looked at me. He leaned over and whispered something to another NCO. I could feel eyes looking at me and then a roar of laughter. I knew instantly that the laughter was at my expense. I didn't like it one iota, but what could I do? If I approached them to tell them what I thought, I could find myself in more trouble than I was already in. So I let things lie as they were and swallowed my pride, coward that I am.

The journey seemed to take ages, what with the train appearing to stop every few minutes. Eventually the troop train arrived at Bridgnorth. It was approximately 22.00 hours. Apart from military personnel at the station, there didn't appear to be any general public about. It looked just as if the station had been closed to the public. As we got off the train, there was mayhem. All I could hear were people shouting from one part of the station, or the other. The whole of the covered railway station echoed with the commands being shouted out. We were ushered outside, and onto a long stream of coaches, all the time being shouted and bawled at. Once we were on board, and the coach was full, it left for the camp, wherever that was. It didn't wait for the other coaches to fill up. Everywhere appeared to be exceptionally dark that evening. None of us knew where we were. It didn't take long for the coach to arrive at our new home.

As the coach stopped amongst the others that had arrived in front of us, I could hear a lot of shouting and swearing. 'Come on, come on, you bleeding lot. Move-it, move-it,' I could hear. 'You're not at home now, you load of nancy-boys. Move-it, at the double,' was the screaming command. We were shepherded into a long aisle, or corridor, like a load of sheep. In the corridor were some more NCOs pushing about twenty recruits into the nearest billet doorway. 'Come on, come on. We ain't got all night. Move it.' Then moving down the corridor to the next door, and so on. Once I had been pushed into a billet, we were left to select our own pit (bed). Each one of us was tired and confused, with the treatment that had been meted out to us. We had been shouted at, and bawled at, and shown no mercy since we had arrived at the camp not more than 30 minutes before. As we were all unpacking at the bedside each had chosen, no one seemed to be in a talking mood, partly because we did not know one another.

'Well, mates. This looks as if this is where we'll be for the next few days until they move us again,' said one of the inmates, to break the silence. 'While we're unpacking, we might as well introduce our-selves,' he added. 'I'm Ted' said the voice, with a very strong southern Irish brogue. 'I'm from Dublin.'

'I'm from Ireland as well. My name's Pete.'

'Oh, I'm from Birmingham,' said another voice. 'And me,' said another, with a very strong Brummie accent.

All told, there were three lads from the Irish Republic and three from Northern Ireland, six from Scotland, three from Birmingham, one from Liverpool, Bristol, Sunderland, Droitwich, Lancaster, Sheffield and Whitley Bay, in Northumberland. Some were National Servicemen, but quite a few had signed up for between three and twenty-odd years.

After about an half hour had passed and we were getting to know one another, the door at the opposite end of the billet flew open, crashing against the wall.

'STAND BY YOUR BEDS,' was the command as two Corporals appeared at the door. They appeared slightly the worse for drink. At least that was the appearance given, whether they were or not I shall never know. Everyone in the room stood, or sat motionless, as if completely mesmerised.

One of the NCOs walked up through the billet. 'Don't just stand there,' he bawled out. 'When a Corporal comes into your room, airmen,' he paused. 'Don't you know what to do?' he queried

Turning to his counterpart who was leaning against the door with his arms folded, he nodded and then grinning, said quietly to one of the recruits nearest him who was seated. 'Don't you know what to do when a Corporal comes into your Billet.'

'No sir,' said the recruit.

At those words, the Corporal continued slowly, as if in a fit of disbelief, 'No sir! No sir!' emphasising the word 'sir.' Then with his voice gradually getting louder and faster as if he was about to explode, 'Laddie, I'm not an Officer. I'm not likely to be an Officer. I don't want to be an Officer,' he screamed, looking towards his mate at the door.

The other continued, 'We're Corporals, with two stripes down our arm,' pointing to his sleeve. 'You don't call us SIR!' he bellowed. 'We're better than Officers. We're your keepers, and when we tell you to jump, you JUMP,' he screamed

'You just call us Corporal,' the first NCO interrupted very quietly. 'When we come into your billet, the first person to see a Corporal, any Corporal, come to that. He will come to attention and shout.'

'CORPORAL PRESENT,' shouted the other as if in a frenzy.

'We couldn't care less if you're bollock naked. You will all – ALL,' he emphasised, 'come to attention. IS THAT UNDERSTOOD?' he bellowed again.

'So what are you doing sat down, Laddie,' said the NCO, who was in the middle of the billet. 'COME TO ATTENTION, AIRMAN,' he bellowed, almost in the poor chap's ear.

The Airman stood up from his bed, not knowing what had hit him.

'We got the lowest of the low, with this lot,' the other Corporal said. 'What are we going to do with this load of shit?' he said mockingly, whilst at the same time, shaking his head as if in absolute disgust.

With that, they went out of the billet, slamming the door behind them. I'm sure I could hear them giggling as they went on their way. 'What's with this bloody lot here?' asked Jock Kelly. 'they're all bloody drunk, or mad,' he finished, exasperated.

'I reckon they're taking the piss out of us,' said Rod from Sheffield in his broad Yorkshire accent.

'Come on you lot,' said Kevin from Whitley Bay. 'Let's get to bed. I've just about had enough of today, what with the shouting and bawling and all the rest.' We all agreed that day was a day best forgotten. Little did we realise this was only the beginning. By the end of the week, some would be in tears and completely homesick.

CLANG, CLANG, CLANG.

'Wakey wakey. Rise and shine. Out of those wanking pits.' We were all woken out of our uneasy sleep unceremoniously. Someone had opened the door and started to bang on one of two metal chimneys from the coke stoves which were situated either end of the billet.

'You have exactly one hour to wash, shave and get your breakfast in the mess across the road,' came the order from the person that had woken us up. Some of the inmates stirred and got up more or less straight away, and some just turned over and went back to sleep. 'Come on, you lot,' came a call, in a Scots accent. 'We don't want any more of last night, do we?' It was Don McDonald, trying to stir the odd one or two out of bed.

Everyone moaned at having to get up.

'What's the time?' came a call.

'Oh it's just five thirty,' was the reply.

'Five thirty. Bloody hell! Who woke us up at this unearthly time?' said another.

I chipped in with a cocky air. 'Five thirty. That's nothing. You want to get up at four o'clock in the morning to be in at five fifteen.' Although still feeling tired, I was already on my way to next door to the washroom. I was fortunate that I was used to being up early in the mornings.

'Aye! Don't know what you Sassenachs would do if you had a farm to run,' called out Rod McBain, who we found out the night before was a farm hand.

Phil James, who was from Birmingham, sarcastically said, 'You lot are out of your bleeding minds,' as he pulled the sheets back over himself. It was a typical cold October morning, as I went to the washroom for the first time. There was a row of old wash basins with two individual taps fixed to each one, one for hot and one for cold water. There was also another row of basins on the opposite wall. On the wall facing each basin, was a mirror for us to watch ourselves shave. I went to the first basin and put my towel and soap at the side, turned on the hot tap and waited a little for the water to become warm. After a while I put my hands under the flowing water to wash. 'Bleeding hell,' I shouted out loud. 'This water is freezing!' We had to wash in cold water. The washroom wasn't exactly a plush place. It was cold and spartan. On the inside of the windows I saw frost. As I cried out, a couple of the others came into the washroom.

'Hells bells, we got to put up with this,' came the cry from another new recruit. As each recruit washed, there were cries of anguish when each one felt the freezing water. By now Jock McBane and I had washed and shaved after a fashion in the cold water. We were both on our way back to our individual bedsides. 'Hark at that lot in there! Jock,' I said, all the time hurrying to get dressed so as to get warm. The billet was only bearably warm, due to the residue of the warmth of the bodies during the night. We had no fire lit at the time.

'Aye, It's a bit bitter for some of them,' he agreed.

By the time the last one had washed, Jock McBain and a few of us were on our way across the road to get some warm breakfast, hoping that this morning was going to be a lot better than the last twenty four hours. After breakfast, and a nice warm cup of tea most of us had managed to get back to the billet within the hour that had been stipulated. As we sat on our beds awaiting the next move we all started to get to know one another a little better. In the billet there was a real mixed bunch of blokes. As I said earlier. There was a farmer's hand; there was also a vicar's son, a carpenter, baker and just about every type in assorted as a bag that one could have. In through the door came a Corporal whom none of us had seen before. He was a well built man – tall, but a little stocky.

'Stand by your beds, Corporal present,' came a small voice from the end of the billet, sounding not too sure whether he was doing the correct thing.

We all came to attention.

'My name is Corporal Anderson, and I have the unenviable job of trying to make you all airmen. I see that you have learnt already,' he added. 'Now line up in lines of three outside on the road,' he ordered quietly. As we came out onto the road to line up with the others I noticed that another Corporal stood outside. 'Move it, move it' he was screaming as each one of us came out of the door.

We lined up. 'Attention. Stand at ease,' was the order. 'My name is Corporal Boon.'

'Oh no,' I grunted under my breath. 'Not him.'

'I expect some of you will have met me,' he looked at me with a great big evil smile on his face. 'But most of you will not have,' he continued.

'Corporal Anderson and I have the most unenviable task of being your Drill Instructors. We both have the most unfortunate job of trying to make airmen of you,' he started again. 'I'm known as the local BASTARD in this camp, and when I say jump.'

Here we go again! I thought.

'YOU JUMP! Is that understood?' he screamed. 'We are going to teach you how to do everything. You're going to learn everything as if you've only just left your mother's womb,' he continued. 'We are going to teach you how to wash, shave, shit, dress, and' he paused, 'we are going to be your mummy, daddy and your father confessor,' he said mockingly. 'We are going to teach you how to make your bed, march, drill, and just about everything there is to learn. By the time we have finished with you you're going to wish you could climb *back* up into your mother's womb, and never come out again.'

What have we got here? A madman, I was thinking. What have I done to deserve this?

'Whatever you have learned before you came here FORGET IT,' he screamed. 'You are going to be the best flight in this squadron. No one, I repeat NO ONE's going to beat my flight. They haven't yet. AND THEY AIN'T GOING TO ON MY LAST FLIGHT EITHER.'

All the time he was ranting and raving Corporal Anderson was stood to one side, just watching us not at all concerned whatsoever. If anything, he had a broad smirk on his face.

'The first lesson is right now,' Corporal Boon started up again. 'When I say ATTENTION, you come to attention.'

'Right! Flight AHH-TEN-TION!' he screamed again.

Everyone came to attention, their hobnail boots clattering onto the road, but not as one.

A few of the recruits nodded in agreement, or just said yes quietly.

Corporal Boon came in again, in his nasty, sarcastically screaming voice. 'When you speak to or answer us you finish with the word CORPORAL.'

'Yes Corporal, no Corporal, three bags full Corporal. Is that understood?' he screamed again. His eyes were just the same, bulging out and he appeared to be frothing at the mouth. There was no doubt that we were in for a really rough ride with this one. 'And you shout it out together. DO I MAKE MYSELF CLEAR?'

'Yes, Corporal.' everyone shouted in unison for his benefit.

'Good,' Corporal Anderson answered. He started again.

'Flight, Ahhhh-ten-tion.'

'ONE, TWO.' Everyone did as they were told, not wanting to upset our new masters.

For about an half hour, we were kept on the road, being brought to attention, and then put at ease, only for it to be repeated over and over again. Most of the orders were being shouted out by Corporal Boon, whilst Corporal Anderson walked around us putting us right by ridiculing us individually. If anyone as much as made a murmur, he was pounced on unmercifully.

'Stop that talking. Look in front of you. You move a muscle and I'll have your guts for garters,' or, 'I'll make you wish you had never been born, you horrible little man.' Anything to ridicule us, seemed to be the 'in' thing. Another favourite was to make us feel an idiot in front of everyone. 'You're a lousy dirty little good-for-nothing nancy boy. What are you, Airman?'

'I'm a lousy dirty little good-for-nothing nancy boy, Corporal' one would have to repeat out loudly. So that everyone could hear you.

'Right! – Now that we can come to attention, we will now start to teach you how to march and halt. When we have done that, we will then take you *all* for your first haircut,' shouted Corporal Boon.

Corporal Boon came up behind one of the raw recruits who had longish hair. Quietly, standing behind him, he said, 'Am I hurting you laddie?'

'No, Corporal,' said the squaddie, not knowing what he was talking about.

'Then I should be laddie, because,' then with a bellow that could be heard around the camp. 'I'M STANDING ON YOUR BLEEDING HAIR. YOU'RE GOING TO GET YOUR BLEEDIN' HAIR CUT. AREN'T YOU AIRMAN?'

'Yes, Corporal,' replied the recruit.

Everyone started to laugh.

'What are you lot laughing about, eh!' bawled the demented Corporal Boon as if the Flight were laughing at him. 'Its no bloody laughing matter. You scruffy load of poofs. If you lot think you're in the Royal Air Force for a good time then think again,' he shouted out to all of us. 'When I've finished with you lot you'll wish you'd never been a twinkle in your old man's balls, you horrible little men.'

Talk about little! The Corporal was no more than five foot tall himself, but he certainly made up for it with his mouth. The bastard, I thought. He was a man whom I had taken an instant dislike to.

After about an hour of being marched, halted and about-turned up and down the road where our billet was, we were marched to the barber's.

Here we were lined up outside; our NCOs told us that we could have any hairstyle we wanted. This brought a smile to one or two long-haired individuals. Oh, its not going to be as bad then, they were thinking. I, for one had my doubts. I was already feeling really demoralised by the grilling we were getting. We were being made to feel inhuman just like cattle being led to the slaughter again. I was feeling lower and lower as the day went on. We had been told that this would be our treatment for TEN WHOLE WEEKS. We were being sent into the barber's, like Noah's animals, two by two. But we didn't come out the same way. When it was my turn to go in, I noticed that there was a lot of hair on the floor. As I was one of the last to go in, this wasn't surprising.

'The usual, Airman?' the barber asked pleasantly, as he put the sheet around my neck. Before I could answer 'yes please,' the electric shears were doing the light fantastic around my neck and over my ears. I had been shorn like a lamb. 'Next!' was the shout as the sheet was taken away from my neck in less than one minute flat. I went outside where the others were standing in the road. I had never seen so many white necks in all my life. Some were feeling the cold, as quite a lot of their hair had been shorn off. They were moaning. I remember it was the very first real laugh I'd had since being in this contemptible camp of ours. I also remember being told what would happen by my mates at work, who had come back out of the services. I could really see the funny side of it. I remember laughing so much as some of the others were doing, partly because of the funny side of it, and also as it was an excuse to release some of our pent-up frustration, without showing our true feelings at the way we were being treated.

During the afternoon, we were shown how to make our beds up ready for inspection next day. We were also shown how to 'bull up' our boots, with spit and black shoe polish, blanco our webbing belts with brushes, and use a 'housewife'.

A 'housewife' was a small sewing pack, with a sewing needle, cotton, wool, to sew any buttons that might come off, or darn, if a hole appeared in your socks.

We had all been issued with these items at Cardington. At the time of issue we didn't know what some of the items were for. When we asked we were told, 'You'll find out!' And indeed, during the next few days we were to discover what all the items of equipment were for. We were not in want for anything as regards cleaning equipment. In the billet was a 'bumper' for polishing the linoleum, which was placed on the floor of the billet. The 'bumper' was a heavy metal block with a broom handle attached to it. Then a rag, or duster, had to be wrapped around the metal block, so that it polished up the floor like glass.

For the next few weeks, we were to be grilled, drilled, shouted at, and generally humiliated by our masters. Invariably we were all dressed from top to toe with a beret on our heads, in a blue denim boilersuit with our webbing belt around our waists, with shirt and tie underneath and gaiters around our ankles which covered the tops of our boots.

We gradually began to get fit with physical training in one of the hangars, and thanks to running around the camp every day. We also began to become a team that would never let each other down, because, if you let yourself down, you would let everyone down. We were being moulded into thinking of each other rather than ourselves. The drilling and general bawling seemed to become part of everyday life, and we began not to take so much notice of it. In fact, we began to have a few laughs – but not in front of our mentors.

I remember after the first week of being shouted at, and being generally humiliated, I was at my lowest ebb. We were told that we were confined to barracks for the weekend and that we were to 'bull up' our equipment, ready for the Monday. During the Sunday morning and afternoon, everyone was busy doing up their kit. We had all just about had enough of it. Quite a few of us were near to tears, and couldn't take much more of the treatment that was being bludgeoned onto us, when in came another lad from an earlier intake who had been at RAF Bridgnorth for about four weeks. He poked his head around the door.

'There's a coach going to Kidderminster at six o'clock for a church service. It's to the Sally Army place. Anyone who wants to come, be ready on the barrack square at 17.45.' With that, he was gone.

A couple of us didn't know whether to go or not. I was in no fit state to think. I had all this work to get ready by the next morning. I was frightened and confused. I wanted to get out of the camp, yet, I didn't know what to do.

BOLLOCKS TO IT, I thought. I've had enough of it. I'm going. ANYTHING TO GET OUT OF HERE. With that thought, I got myself ready, and went out onto the barrack square. I didn't know whether I was allowed out or not, but I was going. I got onto the coach with a few other lads, and off we went.

It was the first time that I had seen civilisation for about three weeks, counting the time that I had been at Cardington as well. It felt good to be out of that confounded prison camp. I was not a religious man, and had never been to church since I was a boy at Sunday school, which was at the age of eleven to twelve years, but I felt I'd do anything to get out of the camp, as I said before.

We arrived at Kidderminster and were ushered into the Salvation Army church. As we entered the church we were greeted and given a welcoming handshake. How different it was from the environment that I had just come from. Were these real people, or was I in a dream? We were ushered to a pew, where we found hymn books. During the evening, the congregation sang. We listened to a choir, and we had a sermon. I couldn't talk, sing or say anything because I felt so emotionally drained. If anything, it was the only time in my whole service life I was to be very near to tears. For some unknown reason, being amongst civilian people appeared to lift my spirits. Or, was it that I was glad to be out of that prison that nevertheless I had to go back too. It was something that I shall never really fathom out.

After about the fourth week, we were issued with 303 Lee Enfield rifles. We were drilled unmercifully with rifle drill, as usual all commands were to be carried out by shouting the timing out in unison, which was to the count of two.

'Flight Ahh-ten-tion.' 'One, Two.' No matter what we did, we had to shout together 'One, two,' bringing our right foot down as hard as we could, so as to make the whole camp hear the hobnail boots crash down onto the floor in unison. Nothing but complete synchronisation was accepted. Your feet were to come down as one.

'Left turn, right turn, about turn.' No matter what the order 'One, two.'

If we as much as moved before the last syllable of the order. For instance, for the order 'Attention,' the action was to be taken at the syllable 'tion.' So 'Ahh-ten-*tion*.' You moved on the last syllable. You move before, you would be screamed at 'AS YOU WERE.' Or, if the NCOs could sense someone was about to move, they would interrupt the order with, 'W-a-i-t for it, W-a-i-t for it.'

It was nothing to hear 'Flight. Slope, (Wait for it, Wait for it,) Arms', you moved and it was a bawling out in front of your mates.

I remember one particular order, which was found to be very hard to get correct. This was the fixing of bayonets. At the order of 'Flight, f-i-x b-a-aynets.' Everyone's bayonet would click into place with individual clicks, rather than as one. Our mentors used to go raving mad. No matter how hard we practised to get this manoeuvre correct, someone or other would add the additional click by coming in that little bit later. It took us several days. In fact our teachers almost gave up the ghost of trying to get us to do it correctly. They used to become maniacal with us. Whoever got the timing wrong would get a bawling out for a hell of a long time. But eventually our timing did come together, and we got it down to a fine art.

Another thing that our mentors did take very seriously, and understandably, was that if an Airman had not fixed his bayonet properly and it had fallen to the floor all hell would be let loose.

'You, Airman, are the biggest prick that's ever been allowed to come onto this earth,' cried a very angry Corporal Anderson, one afternoon. He was screaming right into the Airman's face. It was the only time that I ever saw Corporal Anderson really get angry – and I mean Angry. I'm sure if he could have hit the Airman he would have.

'You're the biggest louse that ever came onto this earth.' Corporal Anderson had given the order to 'slope arms'. This was just after the order to fix bayonets. 'For that you can have a whole week's jankers, cleaning out the Duty Officer's office,' cried out Corporal Anderson. The bayonet had come off the end of the rifle, as the Airman had sloped his rifle onto his shoulder, and had flown through the air, and just missed the head of the Airman who was standing behind him. The bayonet could quite as easily gone into the other Airman's eye, so you can understand why bayonets were not to be trifled with, and that our mentors took things very, very seriously indeed.

On the Friday morning of the fourth week of square-bashing, we were informed that we would be having our first forty-eight hour pass. Before we were to have it, however, we were told, that our webbing belts had to be boiled clean and white on our return from leave. We also had an appointment with the Medical Officer for the first of a series of injections. These injections were known as the dreaded TABT. It was to be several injections in one, and known to be only twenty-five per cent dosage. The second injection, which was to be later on during our stay at RAF Bridgnorth would be seventy-five per cent. On the Friday morning, the Flight (which consisted of the occupants of our hut) were marched to the MO. We were lined up in single file inside the MO's hut to await the doctor to give us the injection. Obviously some of the Flight were apprehensive about this and didn't want to have it. We were now at the stage where we did as we were told, without question.

The doctor came along the line with a male nurse at his side carrying the injection needles. We were ordered to pull up our sleeves and put our right hand on our hips, like a load of nancies, there were no explanations or words of encouragement, like 'Don't worry. It won't hurt' or anything like that. The injections were administered like a production line. As each Airman was given his injection there weren't many grunts, or groans, since the injection didn't hurt as much as expected. After the injections, we were to line up outside in threes as was usual to be marched back to our billet.

'Flight, quick march.' The order was given, after everyone had their injection. None of us felt too bad. We had approximately half a mile to march back to our billet.

Suddenly, just in front of me, Jock Stewart collapsed in the road. Before he could hit the ground (fortunately he was in the middle row) the lads on each side of him caught him and helped him back to the billet. Our mentors told the two lads to take him straight into the billet, and to put him to bed. Of all the people to collapse, Jock, you would have thought would be the last to collapse, the reason being was that he was the Scottish amateur boxing champion for his weight, and probably the fittest of us all. As he was being put to bed, I could see that he was perspiring profusely. Corporal Anderson came in to see if he was alright. He also told us that as from now we were on forty-eight hour leave, and that the coaches left at twelve noon and 17.30 hours that evening for various parts of the country.

After seeing what had happened to Jock, I decided to get my head down in bed, so as to wear off the effects of the injection and catch the 17.30 Coach home.

'AS YOU WERE. AS YOU WERE,' Corporal Boon screamed at us again. He looked towards Corporal Anderson, and said to him sarcastically, 'Corporal Anderson, I don't think much of this sodding lot. They haven't a clue how to come to attention. They're the worst bloody lot of snotty looking layabouts that I have ever laid my eyes on, in my whole bloody life.'

Corporal Anderson nodded in agreement. Corporal Boon marched round to the front of us.

'Right!' he said. 'We'll have to show them how to do it, won't we Corporal Anderson?' Looking over to Corporal Anderson at the same time he said, 'This lot look as if they have only just come out of their bloody mother's wombs. They're absolute rubbish.' He had referred to our mother's wombs yet again. What an uncouth man this is, I thought.

Corporal Anderson came forward, looked at us all, and ordered, 'You will watch Corporal Boon and listen to the order and how it is given.' Turning to Corporal Boon, he gave the order 'Flight'.

'You will notice that the Corporal has not moved, except that he has brought his shoulders back, and is facing the front with his chin up. But you will notice that Corporal Boon is still at ease. 'When you hear the order 'Flight' that is what you do,' Corporal Anderson instructed.

'As you were Corporal,' said Corporal Anderson to his opposite number. 'Flight! Ahh-ten-tion,' Corporal Andrew ordered again.

With that Corporal Boon brought his right knee up and shouted out loud, 'ONE', and then slammed his foot down with great force, beside the other, with hands down to his side. As his foot came crashing down to the ground he shouted out 'TWO'.

'You will notice that Corporal Boon's hands are down to his side with his thumbs to the seams of his trousers,' Corporal Anderson explained. 'And that is how I want to see you do it, AS FROM NOW!' He was suddenly shouting out loud. It was the first time that anyone of us had seen Corporal Anderson get annoyed. 'I also want to hear you shout loudly on every command given to the count of two. The same as Corporal Boon has just done.

'So attention! You shout out loudly "ONE, TWO." Halt! You halt to the count of "ONE TWO." You quick march leading off with your left foot. You come to a halt, starting off with your left foot shouting out ONE, TWO, finishing off at the count of TWO with your right foot. Is that understood?' he shouted.

Chapter Four

Forty-eight Hour Pass

I GOT THE coach that was due to go all the way to Plymouth. It was stopping *en route* at most of the main cities and towns for those passengers who wanted to get off. The same coach would pick us up at stipulated times the following Sunday night on the way back to camp.

I arrived home at approximately 23.00 hours. My parents didn't expect me, as I had not been in contact with them for the period I had been away at Cardington and Bridgnorth. I just hadn't had time to write letters to anyone. As I walked up the front garden path, I noticed that there were no lights on downstairs, or upstairs. They had all gone to bed. I knocked on the front door, saw the upstairs light come on and heard my father shout from the top of the stairs. 'Who is it?'

'It's me!' I replied.

'Who's me?' my father questioned.

'It's Michael,' I said. 'I'm home on a forty-eight hour pass.'

I heard my father grumble something to my mother. After that, the lights came on downstairs. The door opened to let me in. Before I had chance to say 'hello,' my mother welcomed me, not with the words I had expected, but with, 'What are you doing home?' and 'When do you have to go back?' as if I had done something wrong, or I had no right to be home. I said that I had to catch the 22.00 hour coach from near the docks on the Sunday night. We did a little chin-wagging, for about an hour. As we were all tired, we then went to bed.

Next morning, I got up, washed, shaved, and got dressed, putting my uniform on again. I was now proud to wear my RAF uniform.

During breakfast, my father asked how I was getting on in the services. I replied that it was hard going at first, but as I was now getting used to the routine, it wasn't so bad. 'In fact, I'm beginning to enjoy it,' I said.

'Oh! Is that so?' my mother asked inquisitively.

'Yes, we get a few laughs now and then,' I said. I went on to explain some of the experiences that I'd had. During the conversation my mother asked if I had any dirty washing. I said that I didn't have any as the RAF did it for us.

'But they do want me to get my webbing belt boiled white by the time I go back,' I added.

'Come on then. Let me have the belt, I'll try to boil it for you,' my mother offered.

When I gave her my webbing belt out of my holdall my mother was a little surprised to see the thickness of it. 'I don't know how I'm going to boil this,' she said in a rather doubtful way.

'Don't worry then,' came back my reply. 'I'll do it by scrubbing it white.' The family went into rapturous laughter. I wondered what the laughter was all about. 'What's so funny?' I asked, not knowing that I had made an amazing statement.

'You-u-u!' my mother said laughing. 'You wash and scrub your own belt?' The whole family was laughing at my expense. I had forgotten that until now I hadn't done any washing before I went into the services. My mother had done all this for me without my realising, until now. I could now see the joke, and laughed with them.

'Come here. Let me have the belt,' my mother ordered, as she stretched out her hand for me to give her the belt. 'I'll put it in the saucepan to boil.'

My grandfather asked what I intended to do for the day. I replied that I was thinking of going downtown, and into work to see the lads at the office. It was a sort of custom, for the lads that were in the services to go back into work in uniform, to see their workmates, and to tell them of their experiences.

After breakfast, I bulled up my boots, cleaned my brasses, an act which in its way, seemed to fascinate my mother and sister. My mother especially, as she had never seen her only son do such menial jobs before. I put my uniform on, including my peaked cap, and went into the living room, where my grandfather was sitting reading his newspaper while smoking his pipe, as was his habit.

'Ready for inspection Sarge,' I said. 'How do I look then, Pop?' I added, as I came to attention in front of him, and at the same time giving him the best salute that I could muster.

He looked up from his chair, stood up, and then started to walk around me, at the same time giving me an eagle-eyed inspection.

'Not bad. Not bad, soldier,' he said slowly. With a twinkle in his eye, he gave his approval, and then just as I was getting full of confidence, 'but I see they BLACK your boots for you nowadays, my son,' he said, mockingly. If ever there was a knockdown then my grandfather had pulled me down to earth with a great big bump. I noticed that there was still that difference in his attitude towards me, but I couldn't put my finger on it. He treated me as if I were someone different, but at the same time I was still his grandson. It was so strange; there was no hostility in his voice, no menace. He would sometimes come out with comments that only a serviceman would understand. My father and I would laugh at them, whereas my mother and sisters would sit back and wonder what we were talking about. I was in a man's world, talking to my father, and especially my grandfather as one man to another.

That was it! It came to me. I was now in the eyes of my grandfather a man. Not a boy any more. By going into the armed services, I, in my grandfathers eyes' had become a man. So he was now treating me with that added respect.

Whilst on leave, I visited my mates at work. The usual questions were asked that I had asked, while I was waiting to go into the services.

'What's it like?'

'Is it as bad as they say?'

Then, I noticed the inspector coming into the room.

'Hello Baker, how are you. You look fit and well,' he said, with a twinkle in his eye.

'Yes sir,' I replied. 'I feel fit and well.'

'I don't suppose you will be coming back to us then?' he questioned me.

'O-o-oh! I don't know about that,' I said in a rather doubtful manner.

'Well, look after yourself, Baker,' the inspector said. With that he turned and went back into his office.

After I left my old works office I went down into the shopping centre, not for anything special, but just for something to do. I was now beginning to find life in Civvie Street not so interesting, and it seemed there wasn't much going on, especially, during the daytime, because most of my old mates were at work earning their crust of bread. I was finding life a little boring during the day time, and was beginning to wish I was back at camp. Even with the shouting and bawling. At least that was where my new mates were. I was beginning to feel a stranger in Civvie Street. What had become of me to have these strange feelings? Had the services changed me that much in such a short time? It was such an extraordinary emotion. I was feeling fit and well. In fact, I was feeling so fit and well that I wasn't frightened by anything, or anyone. I felt I could take the whole world on, and come out on top. That was something that I had never felt in my whole life before. It was a wonderful feeling.

Chapter Five

Humorous Encounters

ON THE WAY back to camp, after my parents had seen me off at the docks, for some reason or other, I was glad to be on my way. How I could be so mad as to want to go back to this hell hole I just couldn't understand, but I was beginning to enjoy this life in the services after all. It just wasn't comprehensible.

Most of the chaps on the coach were from the earlier intakes and were also in fine fettle. We got back to the camp, some time in the early hours of the morning. I crept into the billet as quietly as I could so that I wouldn't wake those who were asleep. Some of the lads were still not back, especially those that had gone to Scotland, or the North of England. The only ones that had not gone on leave were the fellows from the Irish Republic and I could understand them not going on leave, due to the distance they had to travel home. There was no way that they could have got back inside forty-eight hours. I felt sorry for them. Their lives had been changed out of all recognition, as they had for most of us.

The next morning at five thirty was no different from any other morning routine. Out of bed, wash, shave, breakfast. Fortunately the taps had hot water in them now so life first thing in the morning wasn't so bad. Then there was the usual bulling up the billet ready for inspection. After the billet and kit inspections we were outside in the cold frosty mornings for more square bashing, and after our break for coffee, or tea in the NAAFI. This came at around 11.00 hrs. Then it was time for our proverbial physical training. This consisted of being marched to the far corner of the camp, and then on to a dirt track, between two Ministry of Works workmen's huts and down to a hangar. In the hangar, we would be stripped down to our vest and shorts, given some exercises to warm us up, star jumps, and suchlike, plus running around the inside of the hangar. Once we were reasonably warmed up, we would then come out of the hangar, and run up the dirt track and around the roads of the camp, bearing in mind that we were being bawled at and humiliated by our mentors all the time.

After a week or so of running around the camp I had a definite feeling that there were always one or two of the flight members not present on the run, but they were always there when the run had finished, allegedly just as knackered as everyone else. I just couldn't put my finger on it, but there was definitely something strange going on.

One morning, by sheer coincidence, I found myself at the back of the line of runners. Ben said to me. 'Mike, watch me and the other few at the back and follow.'

'What are you on about?' I asked inquisitively.

'You'll see. But keep your bleeding mouth shut or you'll drop us all in it,' Ben replied.

'Stop that talking in the back there,' shouted out Corporal Boon.

When I looked towards him I'm sure I could see a suspicious expression on his face, as much to say, 'What are you bastards up to.'

We ran out onto the dirt track, up towards the road, and in between the workmen's huts. I noticed that the hut doors were open. As usual, the workmen were in there having a cup of tea. As we ran between the two huts, the rest of the flight went onto the road, but the last four of us peeled off straight into the workmen's hut each side of the dirt track. As the last person got inside the hut the doors were closed before anyone could see what was going on.

I was absolutely flabbergasted at what was happening. If we got caught, we would be on a charge. That's for sure.

'Milk? Sugar?' One workman said to me as if this was a pre-arranged thing, and had been going on for years.

'Don't worry mate,' said another workman. 'They won't be back for at least a half hour. So sit down, and enjoy your break.'

Ben looked up, grinning at me. 'We brought you into it after a comment you made a couple of days ago.'

'Oh yeah! And what was it I was supposed to have said, then?' I questioned.

'When you said in the billet that there didn't seem to be many of us running around the camp.' He was laughing. 'We thought you had cottoned on to what has been going on for a week or so.'

By now there was a nice mug of piping hot tea in my hand. I must say it was the most beautiful mug of tea that I'd had for a long time.

'This is Sam,' introduced Ben. 'It was him who roped us in to start with. We make sure there are only two to four of us at any time. That means that there are two in this hut and two in the hut across the track. Including you, there's only five of us who know about this. So keep your mouth shut. We can't let any more know what's going on.'

'That's right lad. We've all been through what you poor bastards are going through,' Sam started. 'Your Corporals won't say anything, because if they put you on a charge we would only deny any knowledge of this,' he laughed. 'Besides, they haven't a clue of what's going on. Even if they did, they won't want to be made fools of, especially in front of raw recruits.'

Sure enough, about a half hour later the flight was seen to be approaching the workmen's huts. As the runners ran in between the two huts we filtered onto the back of the flight. Back at the hangar we watched the rest of the flight and pretended to be as out of breath as they were.

I said to Ben later on in the day about our encounter as regards the workmen's huts. 'How often do you do this then?'

'Oh! We don't make a habit of it. But we do take it in turns about once a week or so. Otherwise, if we do it too often, we'll more than likely get caught, and we don't want that do we?'

From then on, approximately once, or sometimes twice, every week or two I would be in the hut having a nice mug of tea, whilst the rest of the flight ran around the camp. I always had that gut worry though, all the time I was doing it. Fear of getting caught. But then, as I was so fit now, and my mind was much the same way, I had that feeling as I said earlier that I was no longer frightened of anything, including my mentors. 'If I get caught, I get caught. So what!'

It is said that when a group of men get together for any length of time you will always find at least one comedian, one barrack-room lawyer, one misery. Also, one who keeps himself to himself, the quiet type, and of course one who when it comes to marching, always has two left feet. We had all of these, plus more. Phil was the one with two

left feet, plus two left arms – and two left of everything when it came
to marching. No matter what he did, it was never correct. Our
mentors used him as a punch bag when it came to drill. They would
shout, bawl, and generally humiliate him in everything that he did.
They would shout at the rest of us, or whoever it was standing at the
back of him.

'If he's out of step then KICK HIM ON THE ANKLES.'

I remember Corporal Anderson pulling Phil to one side, whilst
Corporal Boon took the rest of us onto the barrack square. They tried
to teach him right from the very early stages that marching was an
extension of walking. When I say that he had two left feet and two
left arms when marching, that is a literal explanation. With the order
'By the left, quick march' Phil would start off with his left foot, as the
rest of us would. But, his left arm would also go forward with his left
foot where everyone else's arm would automatically go back. Our
mentors tried everything they could to get him to march. They even
tried to get him to walk normally, as he would. But as soon as he was
told to move his arms up to his shoulders, his arms, for some reason
or other would go back to become in unison with his feet – his left
foot and left arm forward together and then his right foot and arm
together. The rest of the lads when we were off duty in the billet tried
to get him to march. We did all the drills with him. No matter who
tried, it was an impossible task. Our Flight (billet) tried everything, but
to no avail, and we all genuinely felt sorry for him. Towards the end
of our ten weeks at RAF Bridgnorth. I think our NCOs threw in the
towel with him as well.

At least once a week we were given a lesson on one subject or
another, such things as 'The Ranks and the Identification of Officers
from all the different British services,' or 'How to survive if a Nuclear
Explosion takes place.'

One day, we were taken to a classroom and sat down at tables, as
was the usual custom. When the officer came into the room we were
called to order, by being called to attention. The officer came to the
front of the classroom, and gave the order 'At ease'. At that we all sat
down again. He then proceeded to give a talk.

This particular day we were given a lesson on nuclear survival. I
remember being told that once a nuclear bomb had been set off the
following phases would take place. First of all the flash, then the

scorch, blast, vacuum, then the recoil of air going back into the flash area. The recoil of air would more than likely collapse buildings that had not already been flattened by the blast. Once all this had occurred there were then the nuclear gamma rays to contend with. Gamma rays would penetrate virtually everything except lead, which had to be of a certain thickness to give you any chance of survival.

'If you see a nuclear flash you must take cover in the nearest ditch, and if possible a wet or damp place. This will stop you from having flash burns. Never hide behind a wall,' the officer said. 'because if you do the blast will blow the wall down on top of you, and probably injure, or kill you. If that didn't kill you, the vacuum from the after-blast would suffocate you.

'Failing that, the suction from the air returning to take up the vacuum in the blast area will be like a blast in the opposite direction,' he said.

I had to grin to myself because no matter what you were advised to do you had virtually no chance of survival anyway if you were within a certain area of a nuclear explosion, unless you jumped into a river. That's if the river didn't dry up. You would probably survive all the burns, blasts and after-blasts etc, only to die of gamma rays (or radiation poisoning, as it is sometimes known nowadays). Unless, that is, you were in a thick lead-lined room, which the gamma rays cannot penetrate. This was if the blast didn't also blow the room away. I thought to myself, why are they telling us all this. We don't stand an earthly anyway.

In the early days of our square-bashing one would not know the difference between a Commissioned Officer and a Senior Non-Commissioned Officer. (Flight Sergeants and Warrant Officers.) We were all very confused, to who, we saluted, and whom we did not salute. So to be on the safe side, we saluted any Officer, or anyone who looked like an Officer that we marched past. I remember my first encounter well.

I was walking along the road towards the NAAFI with Kevin, with whom I had now teamed up. As we passed an Officer, we both marched upright and did the best salute that we could muster. Just as we got past him we heard a bellow that I shall never forget.

'Halt! you Airmen,' came the order from the Officer whom we had just passed.

We halted immediately. 'What have we done now?' we both thought, as we looked at each other. The Officer came up to us. 'Why did you salute me, Airmen?' he asked, as he stood in an admonishing posture, his fists resting on his hips.

'I'm not an Officer,' he continued pointing to a badge on his arm. 'I'm a Warrant Officer. I don't have rings around my sleeves, or strips across my epaulets so don't salute me again,' he admonished.

With that he was on his way. Both Kevin and I just looked at each other, and together we both shrugged our shoulders as much as to say, Oh well another lesson learned.

We walked on towards the NAAFI to have a cup of tea, only to march past another Officer. Whoever he was.

Once again. 'Halt, you Airmen.'

We halted as commanded. 'Don't you salute an Officer when you see one?' came the admonishment.

'Sorry sir,' said Kevin. 'We have only been here a few days, and we don't know the difference,' he said, adding 'sir' as an afterthought.

'I'm a Flight Lieutenant,' He stated. 'A Flight Lieutenant has two rings on his sleeves. A Squadron Leader has two and half rings on his sleeve, and so on.'

'Yes sir,' I said. 'Sorry sir.'

'Now!' he shouted out. 'How do you salute an Officer?'

We saluted him together as best we could. We spent approximately ten minutes with him, being given instructions on how to salute him and any other Officer whom we might encounter. Once again we were being humiliated in front of each passer-by.

From that day onwards, whenever I saw what looked like an Officer or Warrant Officer come to that, at RAF Bridgnorth or the following camps I went to, I always did my best to avoid passing them. I would turn around, and walk the other way, rather than pass them and have to salute.

We never did get to the NAAFI to have that cup of tea that day.

As time went by at Bridgnorth, the month of November gradually got colder, with the frost getting thicker, and staying white in the mornings.

Each billet had two coke stoves, positioned one at each end of the billet. The colder it became, the more coke we would burn during the evenings whilst we were bulling up, or whatever one would decide to do. We were only allowed two sacks of coke a fortnight.

One particular evening, our billet ran out of coke. We slept alright during that night, but the next night we couldn't burn anything as we simply didn't have anything to burn. We mentioned it to Corporal Anderson next morning. He seemed to be more approachable than the other Corporal. His reply came as quite a surprise.

'If you haven't any coke then use your own initiative,' he said.

That was all the advice we needed. We decided to raid the cook-house that evening once it had become dark enough. Luckily for us the cookhouse was only across the road from our billet. It was decided that four of us in the billet would do the raid to collect the coke while one would be on the look-out from just outside the cookhouse. The cookhouse was also situated on the corner of another road. Another of our lads would be on the look-out from the corner of the road just outside the billet. I was one of the raiding party. Why I was picked, I'll never know.

All aspects of the raid were thoroughly taken into account.

We were finally given the all-clear to go. The four of us ran across the road and into the shadows of the cookhouse. Two of us held the sacks open and the other two loaded the coke with shovels that we had brought with us from the billet. Once we had filled up all the sacks each one of us hauled one bag onto our shoulders to carry back.

'Bloody hell!' cried one chap as he hauled the sack onto his shoulder. 'This bag is bloody heavy for coke, or are these sacks bigger than we anticipated?' I had to admit my bag was just as heavy, but at the time I thought it was just my imagination.

'Come on, you bleeders. Don't matter how heavy they are. Just get them back to the billet,' someone else said. We got back to the billet, feeling pleased that we had got away with the raid without being seen or caught. But then we opened the sacks only to find that it was not coke at all. 'No wonder these sacks were bloody heavy. We ain't got coke, but anthracite,' said one of the members of the hut.

'Don't matter about it being anthracite, just light the bloody fires! It's beginning to get a bit cold in here,' said Phil.

The fires were lit, and we all had a lovely hot billet that night. In fact, I wouldn't have been at all surprised if we didn't have the warmest hut in the whole camp because at times the flames were going up the metal chimneys a fair way. We got to bed all feeling proud of ourselves, and went off to sleep feeling warm and snug for the first time since we had been at RAF Bridgnorth.

Next morning, pandemonium was let loose. We had an Officers' kit inspection that morning, and everything had to be spick and span. The floor had to look like glass, all the kit had to be in tip top order, and nothing, but nothing had to be out of order. No dust had to be found anywhere, not even as much as in a crack or cranny. Just nowhere. Of course a lot of our kit had been prepared the night before, whilst we were nice and warm around the fire.

Bert from Birmingham, saw the fire first.

'Hells bells!! Look at those f*****g stoves!' he cried.

The fires, or stoves as they were in actual fact, instead of being black from the liquid blacking we gave them every day, had burnt themselves completely white from the heat of the anthracite. Not only had the stoves burnt white, but so had half-way up the chimney as well. Two of us went to start on blacking the stoves, only to find that we could not do so, due to the stoves still being very hot.

'What are we going to do?' I cried. 'If the bleeding Officers find the stove white like this we'll all be in the shit for bloody months. God knows what Boon will bloody well say.' We were more scared of Corporal Boon than anyone else.

We were stuck. We all tried to find ways of getting the stoves black, but no matter what we tried the stoves would only stay white. At last it was decided to come clean, and say what we had done the night before.

We tidied up around the stove area, putting the poker and other utensils where they were supposed to be, and waited for the inspection, all with fearful trepidation in our hearts.

The door was flung open, as was the norm when an inspection was to take place. In came Corporal Boon. 'Stand by your beds. Officer present,' came the command.

We all came to attention, and stood by our beds, quietly shaking in our boots, fearful of what would be said when the stoves were seen. The Officer came in, looked over each one of our kits, that had been laid out on our beds. Pointed out one or two misdemeanours, just to make sure we were kept on our toes. Put his hand across the top of the door, to make sure there was no dust up there and also felt across one of the window sills for the same reason.

'Fine,' I heard him say to Corporal Boon, and then was gone.

We all sighed a sigh of relief. He hadn't seen the stove, or if he had he didn't say anything. All that worry for nothing I thought.

A few moments went by. Then the door crashed open. In came Corporal Boon.

He was livid.

'If the Officer didn't see the stoves,' he bellowed, 'I bloody well did.' He was going red in the face he was so annoyed.

'I don't want to see these stoves like this again. GET THEM BLOODY WELL CLEANED BY TONIGHT,' he shouted.

'But Corporal,' one of the lads in the billet started trying to explain.

'I don't want any excuses. Just get those stoves clean by tonight!' Corporal Boon broke in.

With that he went out of the door, slamming it hard behind him.

'Miserable bastard,' said Kevin

Jock McBain came in. 'Even if he is a miserable bastard, the stoves have still got to be done by tonight, or we're in the shit again.'

The door opened again.

'Corporal present,' came the command. We all came to attention.

It was Corporal Anderson. 'Right lads, outside.'

We all went outside onto the road and lined up, as was the usual routine. Once again we went through a normal day's training, as usual being shouted and bawled at and the usual humiliation.

The evening was the time for us to be dismissed, and have the evening to ourselves. We all dismissed, and went into our billet. On the top of the stove was a fresh tin of blacking for the stoves, and leaning on each side of the stoves were two bags of coke.

'Who brought this in ?' asked Pete.

'I don't know,' I said, 'Anyway, whoever it was must have known that there was no way we could have cleaned the stoves as they are.'

Jock McBain looked up, and said, 'Do you know what, I reckon Anderson must have said something to Boonie, and those two bastards got together, and did something for us for a change. I reckon that's why Boon bawled us out this morning.'

'Well, well, well,' said Brian Close from Droitwich. 'Who'd have thought that old Boon's got a heart.'

Chapter Six

Passing-out Parade

AS THE WEEKS went by life became a little more bearable. We were still being shouted at, orally abused and generally humiliated. It was part of the treatment but we were now what one could generally be called a 'fighting force.' We knew the routine, and backed each other up, no matter what the provocation. As for our mentors, we began to find some of their antics rather on the funny side. We knew what they liked, disliked, and we sometimes set them up just to get them going, even when it was to our disadvantage, more often than not, just by laughing at some of the comments they came out with. We would try our hardest not to laugh, but it was just too much not to, and we would only to be met with: 'What are you laughing at airman?' as they would go literally running to the airman whom they had caught laughing.

We would give the normal answer, 'Nothing Corporal,' and all the time try our best not to giggle in front of them. It really was hard not to laugh, as we could see the funny side. Laughing at them was a cardinal sin. It would invariably land us up with: 'Right! Since you find things so funny you can clean out the Squadrons Office this evening. Can't you, Airman?'

'Yes Corporal,' would be the reply.

'Report at 19.00 hrs to the Squadron Office, AND MAKE SURE THAT ROOM IS SPOTLESS. Is that understood, Airman?'

'Yes Corporal,' we would answer.

While the Corporal was bawling out one person. The rest of the flight would be trying their hardest not to laugh out loud.

It was nothing now to find a couple of us on what was termed jankers for the evening. We didn't have to worry about the bulling of our kit, as it was now a part of the billet's comradeship which had been built up that if anyone who was put on jankers, or was unable to bull up his kit for one reason or the other' the rest of us would muck in and do it for him.

Another thing that had altered during our square-bashing, was that we didn't have to shout out the words 'One, two' on any command now. We would all move as one synchronised formation and all you would hear was the command given. At the command 'Right turn' the flight would turn with our feet coming down as one. We had a pride in ourselves and no one could split us up. Our flight would defend our name by going out of its way to try to be the best in the whole Squadron, which is exactly what Corporal Boon had said on our first day in Bridgnorth.

We were now coming to the end of our term of ten weeks of square-bashing. Each flight was being polished up for the inter-flight drill competition. Obviously, our flight were out to beat all the others. We worked with our mentors to get the best timing for all the separate movements in the drill. The drill competition was to be held in the last few days of our stay at RAF Bridgnorth. We still had to be told where we were to be posted for our trade training. There was also the passing-out parade. This was to be the very last thing we were to do before going our separate ways to do our individual trade training courses at different camps throughout the world.

A couple of weeks after arriving at Bridgnorth I remember going for my trade interview. We were all marched into one of the class-rooms to see the officer, and to find out what type of jobs were available for a lowly National Serviceman. The officer was in a small room just off the classroom and we all went into see him individually. When it was my turn to see him I was to be told by him, 'You have three choices, Airman.' 'They are, Medical Orderly, Cook, or a T/P Operator.'

I didn't want to be a Medical Orderly or a Cook. I didn't know what a T/P operator was, but I certainly wasn't going to show my ignorance.

'I'd like to be a T/P operator please sir,' I volunteered. I hadn't a clue what I was letting myself in for, but it had to be far better than the other two options.

'I understand that you are contemplating signing on, Baker,' the Officer added.

'Yes, sir,' I replied.

'How are you finding life in the RAF nowadays?' he enquired.

'So far, so good, sir, but I would like to find out a little bit more of what life is like operationally first sir, before I commit myself.' Then added, 'If that's alright with you, sir.'

'M-m-m-m-m,' came the reply, as he looked at my papers in front of him. Then he looked up at me and asked, 'If you sign on Baker, and you have the chance of going abroad where would you like to go?' This conversation was sounding more like another one that I'd had not so long ago. I started again.

'Oh I don't know, sir.' Then, as an afterthought. 'I'd like to go away as far away as possible, sir. Possibly as far as the Pacific, sir. Christmas Islands perhaps?' I added questioningly at the end. 'Right, Baker,' the Officer said. 'You will hear later what trade you are to have before you leave RAF Bridgnorth.' The interview was coming to an end. I stood up to attention, saluted the Officer, and at the same time said, 'Thank you, sir,' and left by marching out of the room.

The whole flight was interviewed for the trades that each individual wished to go for, and most of the flight were Airmen that had signed on from three years and upwards, for the maximum duration.

A few days before we were due to leave the camp for good we were called into one of the educational rooms to be told what trade we had been allocated. I was quite surprised at certain trade postings some of the flight had been given. I remember one of them, who had signed on for some twenty years, was posted to a German photographic factory to learn about the photographic trade. The majority were posted to different camps in this country. There were many and varied trades, from airframe mechanics and cooks to male nurses. One Airman went on to be trained as a dentist. I for one had got my wish to be a T/P Operator, being posted to RAF Compton Bassett. I found out that it was the No 1 radio school, which taught wireless and teleprinter operators. So that was what a T/P Operator was – teleprinter Operator. I was to be posted there just after Christmas, and would be trained there till March.

The drill competition was to be held on the last week of our stay at the camp. We were instructed to bull up the night before, and to be in absolutely tip-top condition – not a brass, buckle, or a crease to be out of order – as an inspection was also part of the drill competition.

Next morning, we were lined up as usual. Corporal Anderson inspected us but Corporal Boon was not with him on this occasion. It was most unusual, as we were not being bawled at or humiliated. In fact, Corporal Anderson was quite human, for once.

After giving us all a good inspection and correcting any small misdemeanours, such as straightening our ties, etc, Corporal Anderson called us to stand at ease and began to give us a lecture on what we had done over the last weeks. Then, changing the subject he went on, 'You are now going onto the barrack square. As you know, or have heard, once you leave this camp the camp is to be no more and for this reason alone, you are going to be the best flight that has ever been posted to this camp.' He emphasised the word 'going,' as if he really wanted us to be exactly that. The best.

'Right. Fli-i-i-ght. Atte-e-e-ntion. Ri-i-ght turn.'

'Qui-i-ck march.' With that we were marched off to the barrack square, our hobnail boots striking the ground as one.

On the barrack square we were halted, and then inspected by a number of Officers and SNCOs. Points were appointed, or knocked off for different reasons. After the inspection, we were put through our paces as regards ordinary drill, and then rifle drill. We were on the square for approximately half an hour. Then marched off the square and back to our billet.

'Right lads,' said Corporal Anderson, after halting us, bringing us to attention and then at ease. 'You have been put through your paces over the last few weeks. You have been shouted at, abused, humiliated. You came to this camp and were told you were a rabble – which you were,' he added quickly. 'On the whole,' he went on, 'you have done very well. You did your best and gave it your all, today, I could see that. In fact, I'm proud of all of you and will be pleased to shake your hands at any time. I know Corporal Boon feels the same, but unfortunately cannot be here today due to some problem. I know that he will tell you himself when he sees you next.'

'AC Morse!' called out Corporal Anderson.

'Yes, Corporal,' said Phil Morse.

Corporal Anderson began. 'Morse, you are now about to be posted to another base for your trade training, and then from there you could be posted to anywhere in the world. I, for my part am about to embark on a trip to a little island in the Mediterranean Sea called Cyprus.'

The Corporal continued 'There is a chance – just a chance,' he put his hand up, and indicated with his index finger and thumb close together, 'that we might meet up again one day, somewhere or other. You will more than likely come up to me and say, Corporal Anderson, I was in the very last intake at RAF Bridgnorth where I was in your Flight. Remember me?' Corporal Anderson then took a great breath and bellowed out with all the sound that he could muster. 'THEN DON'T! BECAUSE I WON'T WANT TO KNOW YOU, OR YOUR TWO LEFT FEET.' He then started to grin. We all laughed with him, as we could see he was taking the mick out of poor Phil and his two left feet, which unfortunately lost us the competition.

On the last day of our stay at RAF Bridgnorth, quite a few were feeling excited and pleased to be away from this accursed camp, which some had learnt to really hate. Others were pleased to be going away from the camp, but were in some way sorry to leave to go somewhere into the unknown. The ten weeks had changed all of us in some form or other. We were without doubt fitter than we had ever been, and more confident. I, for one, would remember RAF Bridgnorth for ever. I didn't hate it, as I first thought I would when I came through the gates some weeks earlier. In fact, I rather came to enjoy it, what with the laughs and comradeship. If ever I had been in trouble with our mentors, it was because I was always getting caught laughing at some other erk's misfortune. (Erks was the nickname for all non-commissioned Airmen.) But it was no more than they did, at my misfortunes.

I can always remember the very last misfortune that befell me at Bridgnorth. It was on the actual passing-out parade and that particular morning there was a very severe frost. The whole camp was white with it. We were all as smart as ninepins, dressed in our No 1 uniforms, with overcoats being worn. With our rifles, we were marched onto the parade square, where we were to be inspected by the AOC (Area Officer Commanding).

We went through the usual formalities, like lining up, being brought to attention, sloping arms, etc. Some of the movements were basically just to keep us warm. I realise this now, but at the time I, as many, others, were cursing under our breath at having to carry out all the drill commands. Finally, we were brought to attention. As I looked around me, the whole Squadron could be seen to have

condensation coming from their mouths where it was so cold that
morning.

'Squ-u-u-u-u-ad. Slo-o-o-o-pe arms!' The command was given.
The whole Squadron on the parade ground moved as one. It was a
great feeling to see and hear more than four hundred men move as
one, fifty percent of them, being the biggest and last intake of National
Servicemen. The CO started his inspection of the troops line upon
line. He moved along. As the time went by, I'm sure we were all
getting cold. We had to move our toes inside our boots. There were
one or two Airmen who had grown moustaches. and these were
beginning to go white with the frost. I'm convinced I was not the
only one who was beginning to find the rifle we were holding on our
shoulders getting heavier and heavier. My biceps were beginning to
ache, and I wanted to put the rifle down as quickly as possible. I wish
the bleeding old man would hurry up and finish this inspection, I
began to think. We were stood in this position for between three
quarters of an hour to an hour at least it felt like that at the time. My
arm was by now aching like hell, and I felt as if it was frozen stiff. I
couldn't feel the rifle – my fingers were numb with the cold even
though I had my gloves on. 'Is this what frostbite is like?' I thought.
Then they can keep it.

'Sq-u-u-u-u-ad, O-o-rder Arms,' I could hear everyone else carry
out the order, but I just couldn't move my arm and had to use my
other arm to take the weight of the rifle from my frozen arm. Even
after taking the weight off I still couldn't move my arm from the
forty-five-degree angle that I had been holding the rifle. The ache in
my arm had now become an excruciating pain. Where everyone else
had their rifle in their right hand, by now and resting on the ground,
I had mine in my left hand, my arm still at forty-five degrees. Within
seconds, a Corporal came running up to me. He must have noticed
that I was in difficulty. He took the rifle from me. 'You alright,
Airman?' he enquired. 'No Corporal,' I answered. 'My arm is solid
from the cold. I can't straighten my arm,' I explained. I was by now
trying my best to get my arm straight. I was also beginning to be
embarrassed, and felt that I had let the other lads from my Flight
down. 'I'll be alright in a minute, thanks Corporal,' I said in gratitude.
'It's probably the cramp,' I added. I took the rifle back from him and
brought myself back to the same order as the rest of the parade. At the
same time feeling as embarrassed as could be. We eventually marched

off the parade ground. My arm, although reasonably straight by then, was still aching like hell, and ached for quite some hours after. We were then dismissed, and were generally relieved of such things as our rifles, and other equipment we would no longer require, once we left the camp. We were given approximately a week's leave for Christmas. After our week's leave we were ordered to report to our individual camps at a certain time and date. In my case it was to be RAF Compton Bassett, a camp not far from Calne in Wiltshire.

Chapter Seven

RAF Compton Bassett

THE CHRISTMAS RECESS at home was a very enjoyable interlude. I was able to go and meet my old mates at work, plus a lot of other friends, such as those at the motorcycle club. Obviously, everyone I met was interested in what I had been up to, and how I was getting on in the services. I told them of the funnier sides of life, as well as some of the more harrowing events. I was by now feeling really proud to be a member of Her Majesty's armed services. I would always wear my uniform, even though I could have worn civvies during my stay at home.

My relatives' attitude was different towards me, especially my father and grandfather. I remember one particular day my family insisted (well, my mother did) on having a photo taken of me outside the house at exactly the same spot and the same position as my father had his photo taken many years before, during the Second World War (approximately 1939). Once the photo had been developed I was amazed at how much my father and I resembled each other when in uniform, although, obviously it was father and son, in the two separate photos. We were like the same person, only in different uniforms. My father in his army uniform (RASC) and myself in my RAF uniform.

The day came for me to go to RAF Compton Bassett. As I had to report there by 06.00 hours on the Monday, I decided that it would be best to go there during the Sunday afternoon. My father said it would be a good idea for all of them to go out for an afternoon's drive in the car, and at the same time take me to the camp, Calne not being much more than thirty miles away. I accepted my father's suggestion.

We arrived at Compton Bassett a little after 16.00 hours and we all said our goodbyes, and I left them outside the camp, waving goodbye as I went through the camp gates. I went into the guardroom to report, with some apprehension. As at Bridgnorth, the guardroom was treated as the inner sanctum. No one entered it without a feeling of foreboding, or you had done something wrong, you were due for a right dressing down.

A guardroom's layout is very similar to that of an ordinary police station, which, when you enter it you would come to a counter.

At the counter stood an RAF policeman. 'Yes, Skip! What can I do for you?' the White Cap asked. I was somewhat taken back at the rather civilised and friendly approach.

'I have to report here for trade training tomorrow morning, but decided to come this evening, to save the rush in the morning,' I started.

'Oh yeah!' came the curt reply.

'Where do I have to report, and where do I kip down for the night?' I continued.

'What's your name for a start,' the guard asked, as he pulled a sheet from the table, the table being situated behind him.

'Baker M,' I replied. '5081805', I added, as an afterthought.

The White Cap went down the list he had in front of him with his finger. 'Ah! Yes! Baker M. You just come from Bridgnorth, ain't you?' he stated in a matter-of-fact tone of voice.

'Yes, that's correct,' I said, in answer to his question.

'You're in hut 29, which is over there to the right of the square.' He pointed in the direction I had to go. 'Don't go to the left, or you'll find yourself in trouble, as it's the WRAF's quarters.'

'Thank you' I replied. I picked up my kit bag, and proceeded out of the guardhouse towards the group of huts that stood to the right of the square. I noticed as I walked, that there appeared to be a lot of bicycles and motorcycles parked around, in the old air-raid shelters. Every air-raid shelter had one side wall knocked out so that these motorcycles and bicycles were sheltered from the elements.

I found No 29 hut with little difficulty. I entered to find that the billet had already one or two erks there. 'Hi,' one of the Airmen said, as I entered the hut. 'You just arrived?' What a bloody stupid question to ask, I thought. Here was I, laden down with my kit-bag, and in full uniform and he asks have I just arrived? Not to be vindictive, I just answered 'Yeh! that's right. Which pit do I have?'

'Take your pick,' came the reply. 'We're the only three here at the moment.'

'My name's Andy,' said one of the erks, as he came towards me to take my kit-bag from me. 'I only live a few miles away in Swindon. Colin here lives in Salisbury. So we're more or less local lads, one might say.'

'My name's Mike Baker,' I replied. 'I come from Bristol, which is not far away either. In fact, my old man and mother brought me here in the car. They made it a Sunday afternoon drive out for themselves at the same time.' I started again. 'What trade are you two erks here for?'

Colin answered. 'I'm here for teleprinter operator training.' Then Andy interrupted with 'Yes! well I'm here for a wireless operator's course. You know, Morse Code and all that.'

'I'm here for a T/P course as well,' I came in. 'Perhaps you and I will be in the same class,' I looked towards Colin.

All the time this conversation was going on, I had selected my pit, nearest the stove, and was unpacking my kit-bag. I had no intention of being cold during my stay in this camp, like I had been at Bridgnorth.

Andy asked if any of us were hungry, as the time was approximately 17.30 hrs. We all agreed that we were. So after locking up our belongings we went to find the mess to have a nice warm meal.

I had noticed all the time, since I had entered the camp, there was a different atmosphere. An atmosphere of less tension. No one appeared to be on edge, or seemed to be looking over their shoulders.

We found the mess and entered. For the first time I saw my first members of the WRAF. There was a group of them seated at a table having a meal. A few tables away was another table where some other Airmen were sitting. Andy, Colin and I went over to the serving counter, and helped ourselves to a meal, and then sat down at a vacant table to eat it. The meal itself was very different to what I had come to expect from the RAF. It was a lot better than at Bridgnorth, but still not comparable to home cooking.

After our meal, we all went back to our billet to find that a few more erks had arrived. We introduced ourselves to one another. There were two other fellows who had just come from Bridgnorth, but I had not known them there, as they had been in another flight.

Next morning we were aroused by a Tannoy wishing us a 'Good

morning' and that the time was 06.30 hours. This was a much more civilised hour to be awakened. If this was what RAF life was going to be like in the future then this was going to be the life for me.

We all got up and were met after breakfast by a Flight Sergeant, who had us all outside our billets on the Upper Road. He must have been very near the end of his RAF career, because he was more elderly than most of the SNCOs I had seen before. There was no shouting or bawling, just a quiet order to come to attention, for roll-call, etc. He was a quiet-spoken man and had a rather fatherly appearance, but nevertheless held an air of command and respect. He explained what was expected on the camp, and told us that the weekends would be our own. If any of us lived locally, as long as the camp knew where we were, then it would be in order for us to have weekend passes. However, it was expected that all of us would have to spend at least one weekend on guard duties at the main gate, or somewhere in the camp.

I thought to myself, if this is so, then I can go home this weekend and come back on my motorbike. I saw the Flight Sergeant later on in the day and mentioned what I had in mind. His reply was that as long as I gave him all the details of my home address, and my motorcycle registration number, then he could see no problems. He gave me a chitty to fill out and that was that.

Each morning, after roll-call, we were marched off to our individual classrooms. My particular classroom had typewriters at each table. We were to be taught how to type by a civilian teacher. He told us that the course for a teleprinter operator was a three-month course. We had to learn how to touch-type; read perforated tape; know how to lay out a message, and other procedures. The first few days we were taught to use the top row and the middle row keys on the typewriter. Then, as the week went on, the bottom row of keys was added as well. We were taught how to touch-type using a blind keyboard . This was done by putting a shield over the keyboard so that we could not see the keys we were touching. In time we came to be able to touch-type. The RAF's system for accurate typing was to learn accuracy first, and the speed would come with experience. Later as the weeks went by, we were taken to another classroom where instead of typewriters, teleprinters were installed. Things became even more interesting. We were taught the basic speeds that a teleprinter could handle, and that was a mere percentage of 66.6 digits per minute.

Towards the end of the course I became too fast with my typing for the teleprinter to cope with, and found the messages I typed would become garbled. My instructor told me that, whilst working on a teleprinter, I would have to slow down. However, if I wanted to find out how fast I could go then the perforator could go as fast as I wished it to go.

In the course of time, I found that I was really enjoying the course. I found it really interesting, and what with being able to go home during the weekends, it was really bliss. As soon as the last class finished at around 16.00 hours on the Friday, I was in the billet, changed into my motorcycle gear, and on my motorcycle within half and hour, getting home by approximately 17.30 hours. Having the whole of the weekend off, and leaving home at about 23.00 hours on the Sunday, to be back at camp by approximately midnight.

Then came the week that I wasn't particularly looking forward to. That was the weekend I had been informed about on the first morning at RAF Compton Bassett – guard duties.

We were instructed that we had to report at 18.00 hours on the Friday evening to the Duty Corporal at the guardroom. There was about a dozen erks to do Guard Duty over the weekend. We were informed at the guardroom that we were to do two hours on duty, and four hours off. We were not allowed to go anywhere, but had to stay in the guardroom at all times, except if we were told to do any specific job.

My first job was to be on guard at the main gate in the sentry box, with a rifle. The rifle had five rounds of ammunition, one of which was up the spout. We had to adhere to instructions regardless of provocation, should there be any.

I did my two-hour stint, without any unwarranted problems and was relieved of my guard duty by another erk, whereon I was marched back to the guardroom. I stayed in the guardroom playing cards with some of the other unfortunate Airmen on guard duties, and read some magazines, during my four-hour rest period. I was then detailed to go on guard at the main gate again for another two hours. This went on throughout the night until we were relieved of our duties in the morning.

My stay at Compton Bassett went by very fast, and I knew my time

was coming to an end. Once again, I had an interview with an
Officer, as to how I was enjoying my time in the Royal Air Force.
The usual questions were put to me.

'How was I finding the RAF?'

'Where would I like to go?'

'Would I be signing on?'

The answers were much the same as before, except for the answer
regarding signing on. Here I replied, 'I would more than likely be
doing so, but would like to see what an operational station was like
before actually signing on.'

The day came when we were all taken to an empty classroom,
where an Officer came in to tell us of our postings. There were about
a dozen of us grouped together.

'Right,' said the Officer. 'I will call out your name and last three,'
(last three numbers of your service number.) 'and then the base to
which you will be posted.'

'Amos   – Akrotiri, Cyprus.'
'Ambrose   – Gutersloh, Germany.'
'Bennett   – Khormaksar, Aden.'

Then! 'Baker.'

'Sir,' I replied, as did all the others before me. The Officer went off
on an entirely different track. He started again.

'Baker, well, you are the luckiest man in this group. Your posting
is,' he hesitated, 'Changi.'

'Changi sir? I questioned. 'Where's Changi sir?'

'Don't you know where Changi is Baker?' he replied, as if in utter
astonishment that I didn't know where Changi was.

'No sir,' I replied.

'Changi, Airman, is in Singapore. Apart from that, it is commonly
known as one of the best postings anyone could hope for. You lucky
perisher.'

I'm sure he would have liked to have called me something else . . .

Not even knowing where Singapore was, I came back with 'I beg
your pardon, sir, but, where's Singapore?'

'You don't know where Singapore is?' the Officer gasped in absolute
amazement, that I didn't know where the country was. 'Singapore,
Airman, is in the Far East,' he went on. 'I suggest when you get home
on embarkation leave tomorrow you look at your world atlas, and
familiarise yourself as to where Singapore is, my son.'

The Officer then went on to rest of the group, as before.

'Tarrant – Wildenrath, Germany,'

and so on.

After we had all been told our postings he went on to tell those that were going to postings abroad that we were to report on a specific day to RAF Innsworth, which was in Gloucestershire. Whilst there we would have our photos taken for a passport, and the usual documentation. This would take approximately two to three days. After the documentation, we would be transported to the airport, to be flown out by civilian kite.

I had now been promoted to the high rank of LAC (Leading Aircraftman). This allowed me to wear a badge of two propellers on my sleeve. We had also been issued with our signals flashes, which were to be worn on each shoulder of our sleeve. The flashes consisted of three streaks of lightning held in the centre by a medieval gauntlet. I was now a tradesman but I didn't realise how significant the trade that I had learnt was to be to me in later years, especially the typing aspect.

The next day we were issued with the necessary papers to take to our new base. In my case, this was RAF Innsworth. We were then given three weeks' embarkation leave passes, and dismissed from RAF Compton Bassett.

Chapter Eight

Flight to Singapore

I SPENT MOST of my embarkation leave by visiting workmates, motorcycle club members and relatives, etc. The only advice given to me about going abroad was from my father advising me that whilst in a hot climate, I was to go about my business as normal and not to go sunbathing for more than a quarter of an hour a day to start with, but as I became more acclimatised, to extend my sunbathing by a quarter of an hour at a time, until I would be able to stay out in the sun for as long as I so wished. Failing to adhere to this, he said, I could end up finding myself suffering from sunburn, and on top of that, finding myself being put on a charge for 'self-inflicted wounds'.

The three weeks went by reasonably quickly. I wasn't sorry as I was excited, not so much about going to Singapore but because it would be the very first time that I would be going up in an aircraft – a dream that was coming true. I'd always had this dream, from my days as a boy, whilst watching aircraft fly over our house from the airfield nearby, during the Second World War and after.

As was the case at my earlier camp my father and mother took me to the camp, to see me off and also to make it a day out for themselves. On this occasion it was to the aforementioned RAF Innsworth in Gloucestershire.

I spent about three days there having my passport photo taken, getting medical checks and the usual documentation. When handed to me on my passport I found with some surprise that my occupation was not Royal Air Force personnel, but a government official. We were handed flight tickets and were told that we were to be taken to Stansted Airport to fly by a civilian airline called British United

Airways. The Estimated Departure Time (ETD) was 00.30 hours. We were told that we were to go in civilian clothing, and not in uniform. We were also told that should anything untoward happen during our flight, we were not to disclose that we were members of Her Majesty's Services, only that we were government officials. I found this to be no problem, as I had just come from one civil service section (General Post Office) into another. Should I have to disclose what I did, then I was a civil servant working for the General Post Office.

We didn't have to take any of our RAF blue uniforms, because we had been kitted out with khaki tropical uniforms. Our RAF blue uniforms would be sent out by other means, probably by air a couple of days later. Before being sent, all the blue uniforms had to be mothballed, and sealed against the tropical environment.

On the morning of our departure from Innsworth, we were put into an RAF coach with all the other erks that were going abroad, most of whom were from other camps where they had received their individual trade training, or had been posted before. Although I didn't know any of them I found most had been at RAF Bridgnorth around the same time as I was.

Our first stop in the coach was to be RAF Hendon. After a uneventful journey, we arrived there for an evening meal at approximately 17.00 hours. We were ushered in through the side door of an old hangar. As I came from the light outside it took a few seconds for my eyes to get accustomed to the darkness. We were led past the most amazing line of old aircraft I had ever seen. There were Spitfires, Hawker Hurricanes and bombers of all types, and many other types of aircraft from the Second World War. There were Gloster Meteors, De Havilland Vampires and Venoms, from just after the War. There must have been at least fifty-odd aircraft parked nose to tail as if in mothballs. (I found out many years later that these aircraft were the beginning of the RAF Museum at Hendon.)

We were led between the aircraft, and up some steps into a room where there was a canteen awaiting us with a nice warm meal, and a cup of tea. We spent around two to three hours there. We were not authorised to go anywhere near the aircraft that we had seen as we came in. Most of the airmen just sat around playing cards, reading magazines, or just talking between themselves. I had made an acquaintance with another airman who, was also going to Singapore. His base was to be RAF Seletar. Wherever that was.

Finally, some of the airmen were called, and taken to a coach that was waiting to take them to Stansted Airport. I was one of the party. We were driven through the London suburbs, which was another first for me, as I had never been to London before.

Eventually, we arrived at Stansted Airport. The usual checks were made on our passports, tickets and weight of our baggage. The passengers just sat around after the checks to await the announcement of their individual flights. The excitement grew for me, as over the Tannoy our flight was announced. 'Would passengers for Singapore flight number BUA 1234 please go to Gate number three?' I knew that we were going on the latest type of aircraft, which was a Bristol Britannia, Commonly known as The Whispering Giant. We were assisted to a passenger coach just outside the building, then driven onto the aircraft aprons and taken to the awaiting aircraft. We were welcomed on board the aircraft by the air hostesses, and ushered to our allocated seats. I was fortunate to have a window seat, just in front of the wing, but between the engine nacelle and fuselage so I was able to look down during our flight, not that I was going to see anything, as it was now midnight.

I was in a state of euphoria. Here was I, going on a long journey, some ten thousand odd kilometres, and landing in several countries. The first one in Turkey being at Yesilkoy Airport (Instanbul), then on to Karachi, Bombay and then finally Singapore. I was like a two-year-old. The flight would take, with fuel stops, nearly thirty hours, and here was I on it. I couldn't believe that I wasn't dreaming. It was for real. The engines started up. We were informed to fasten our seat belts, and we were shown the usual safety procedures by the air hostesses. It was all most exciting. We started to roll as we were being given our safety procedures. Finally we got to the end of the runway. The aircraft opened up all engines. The noise was noisier than I expected. Then the brakes were released. We started to roll along the runway with ever increasing speed. I felt as if the back of the seat was being pushed into my back by the sheer brute force of the engines throwing us along the runway. Suddenly the nose of the aircraft lifted, and I found that I was airborne at last.

As we went further into the air I could see the lights of the cities and towns below. Just as I was beginning to enjoy the view of the lights, we went into cloud, as we climbed even further. After going into the cloud the captain of the airliner came on the loudspeaker to inform us that we were to fly at 17,500 feet *en route* to Yesilkoy Airport, and would take four hours to arrive at our first refuelling stop. From there we would be flying on to Karachi, and at a height of 19,500 feet. All this I could hear, but I was too interested in looking out of the window to see if I could spot anything. Of course, we were well above the cloud, and I couldn't see a thing.

We were served a nice warm meal about half an hour after taking off. It consisted of typical English roast beef, Yorkshire pudding, and vegetables, followed by a cake, biscuits, and nice hot cup of coffee or tea, whichever our requirements were. But even during my meal I just couldn't take my eyes away from the window.

After roughly an hour or so of flying the clouds below began to clear and I could see the lights of small towns. Then I was watching the illuminations of an exceptionally large city, where the lights were like a large spider's cobweb.

During the flight Alf, the erk beside me, whom I had befriended earlier, said to me, 'Here Mike! That air hostess that keeps walking up and down with the drinks.'

'Yeah, what about her?' I replied, keeping my eyes still glued to the window, showing no interest whatsoever.

'Well. Every time she walks past us she takes particular notice of you, and sort of grins,' my companion started.

Still looking out of the window I replied, 'Oh Yeah?' Not really taking any notice of his remarks.

'No, honest. The brunette, with longish hair. She's a right corker,' he went on 'I reckon you're onto a winner there, if you play your cards right mate.'

'Oh, a-h-h,' I replied, still with my face fixed to the window, and showing no interest at all. 'You'll be telling me I'll be able to get my end away next,' I replied with a sarcastic tone to my voice.

'No honest. Look, here she comes again. You watch. I bet she looks over towards you,' he retorted.

Not moving my face from the window, because I didn't want to miss anything, I pulled away sufficiently to be able to see the reflection behind. Sure enough, the air hostess came up to us, and asked my companion, 'Would you like anything to drink, sir?'

'If you have a whisky. I wouldn't mind having one, please,' he said to her.

'And what about your friend next to you?' she added. 'Would he like to have something to drink?'

I turned around, and replied, 'Thank you, but not for me,' I looked at her properly. She was without a doubt a real corker. My mouth suddenly became dry. 'On second thoughts, could I have a nice cool drink please. Have you an orange juice please, as I am feeling a little dry.'

I felt rather embarrassed as she went away to get our drinks. 'I told you, Mike. She's got an eye for you. You lucky bastard, you.'

'Piss off, you must be mental or something,' I said, scoffing at him.

'Oh well. Please yourself mate. But don't say I didn't tell you, if you miss out on a good thing, you stupid bugger,' he came back, replying in a mocking attitude.

She came back with our drinks, but nothing more came of it.

We landed at Yesilkoy airport some time around 02.30 hours local time, although we had been flying for about three and a half to four hours; the time difference was due to the time jump. We were taken off the aircraft while it was being refuelled and ushered into a waiting room. As we went into the waiting room. I could smell something that was really obnoxious. I knew I couldn't stay in the room, because of the smell so I decided to go outside, and watch the aircraft being refuelled. I leant against a pillar. I must have been outside watching the aircraft for approximately a quarter of an hour when a female voice came from behind me.

'You're Mike Baker aren't you?' the voice enquired.

'Yes! That's correct,' I replied, as I turned around towards the voice. It was the air hostess, that had been serving us in the aircraft. 'Why aren't you inside with the others?' she asked.

'Oh, there's a smell in there that I don't particularly like. So I've come out here in the fresh air.'

'That smell isn't all that nice, is it,' she retorted. 'But that's the smell of Turkey, I'm afraid,' she added.

'Is it alright to smoke a cigarette out here?' I asked her, at the same time offering her one.

As she took the offered cigarette, she answered, 'I should think so. You're right away from the aircraft. You come from Bristol don't you?' She came straight out with it.

'Yes that's right.' I was somewhat surprised by this statement, but
thought that she may have got it from the flight list.

'You used to go to Cheddar Grove School,' she added.

'Yes. That I did,' I replied, with some surprise. She couldn't have
got that off the flight list. By now my ears had pricked up. How in the
devil did she know that I went to that school?

She then came back. 'You were in Mrs Lloyd's class weren't you?'
The air hostess with the mostest had me absolutely flabbergasted.

'How did you know that?' I was now completely dumbfounded.

She went on with more information. 'And you used to sit at the
back of the class, on the end row next to a girl,' I just nodded. She
went on, 'When you had music lessons, and had to sing, you used to
stand up at the back beside your desk. Remember?'

'How do you know all this?' I was now completely at her mercy.
'How in the hell do you know?' I repeated. I was completely
mesmerised by now.

'Can you remember the name of the girl that you used to sit next
to?' she asked, as if expecting the reply to be correct.

'Yeah, let me think,' I began. 'It wa-a-a-s' . . . I paused, trying to
think of the freckled, short girl that I used to sit next to at school. I
had to think back some twelve, thirteen years. 'Yeah! that's right. It
was a Maure-e-en Sheppard, if I remember,' I came out with the
name slowly, as I was thinking at the same time. By now my mind
was in turmoil. 'Excuse me for asking, but how in the hell do you
know all this about me?'

'Mike Baker! Don't you recognise me?' she asked, grinning from ear to
ear. 'I wondered if it might be you when I saw the flight list and saw
where you came from.' She was full of excitement, as if she had found
a long lost friend. 'I'm Maureen Sheppard, you ninny!' she laughed.
'How many years is it since we used to be at school together?'

'It must be at least thirteen years,' I said, my brain now beginning
to function again. 'You're not *the* Maureen Sheppard, that short, little,
freckled tot that I used to sit next to. Are you?'

'Yes! That's me,' she replied and chuckled, as she put her arms
around me.

She was a real beauty now. What a transformation! She smelt of
perfume. She had no more freckles, or didn't appear to have any and
her long black hair was absolutely glorious. She was absolutely
gorgeous. I could now see how my companion thought I was onto a

good thing, and also why Maureen was looking at me during the flight.

'Come on over here and sit down.' She guided me over to a seat. 'We can sit for another half hour and talk about old times.'

We sat as she said, and talked about the old days, and about different school kids that we knew and wondered what had become of them and what had happened to the different teachers and so on. I asked her if she was going all the way to Singapore. She said that she was only going as far as Bombay, then had a day off there, and was to fly back to Britain. Our time came and went very fast and she had to go before the rest of the passengers were sent for. We got on the aircraft again after it had refuelled. Alf asked where I had been, as he hadn't seen me in the waiting room.

'Oh, I stayed outside and watched the aircraft being refuelled. I didn't like the smell inside the waiting room.'

'No, it wasn't all that nice was it,' he replied. The subject was then dropped.

'Oh, by the way,' I said, as we began to fasten our seat belts, 'that air hostess was talking to me,' Alf looked up in astonishment.

'Was I right about her? Did she have an eye for you?' he asked inquisitively.

'You could say that,' I replied. 'I'll tell you something else,' I went on. 'She's only going as far as Bombay. But we shall be well looked after from now on,' I added.

'You crafty old bastard. You scored then?' he started. 'You crafty old git. Here was I thinking you were a bit of idiot not taking up a chance like that. Well, you scheming devious little bleeder.'

Then Maureen came along the aircraft checking the passengers had their seat-belt fastened. Winking at me and smiling, she said 'You have your seat-belt fastened, sir?' as she looked at Alf's belt. 'Yes thank you,' he replied. She leant over Alf, as if to check that I had my seat-belt fitted correctly. 'I'll see you later on, Mike, once everyone has settled down for the rest of the flight,' she whispered. Alf couldn't believe his ears. I, in turn, just grinned, and thought to myself, there's no way that he's going to know that Maureen and I are old school friends. I'll let him think what he wants to think. Needless to say, I had a very enjoyable flight and couldn't put a foot wrong. I also found that the other air hostesses were looking after Alf and myself a little more than usual. I'm sure that Maureen had put the word out.

During the flight we had been informed by the captain that we would
not be landing at Karachi, since there were no passengers due to leave,
or be picked up, so the aircraft would be flying onto Bombay non-
stop. We would be arriving at six in the evening, local time. I was a
little disappointed, as it meant that I would not have much of chance
for another little chat with Maureen on the ground.

The hours went by, and I remember flying over what I took to be
the edge of the Himalayas. We were flying, so we were told, at 19,500
feet. The mountains were coming up very close to us. We couldn't
have been more than a thousand feet above the mountains at times.

All of a sudden the aircraft seemed to be meeting the ground, as the
mountains appeared to come up to the aircraft. First came the mountain range with the grey granite, then green pasture, as if they were a
belt above the rocks. The pastures were a lush light green, like the
green of moss – soft and delicate. The ground was now coming up
even closer. All of a sudden the plane's wings were below the mountain peaks. I could see the lush green grass more clearly followed by a
distinct line of snow, which went on up to the top of the mountain
peaks. Below the snow line I could see a shepherd minding his sheep.
He was looking up towards us, shielding his eyes against the bright sky
and waving to us, as if we were some long lost friends, and the only
living thing for miles around, we were that low, we were in actual fact
flying between a mountain pass at around 19,500 feet as the captain
had said. I only wished that I had a camera with me. No sooner had
the mountain been above us, than it began to fall away below us, and
it seemed as if we were climbing again.

As the flight came closer to Bombay it was announced that the
temperature outside was eighty degrees Fahrenheit. I felt confident of
myself. 'Oh, that's not too bad. I think I can cope with that type of
heat.'

As the aircraft came in to land at Bombay approximately two to
three hundred feet above the runway I saw for the first time what
poverty was all about. Set to the side of the runway perimeter were
some small huts made from four posts covered with palm tree leaves,
or the like. They appeared to be no higher than four feet tall by four
feet in width. Standing at the side of one of the huts was an Indian
woman in a decrepit and tattered sarong. Smoke was coming out of
the side of the hut. Surrounding the hut was nothing but mud and
waste, with chickens and goats going in and out of the huts. I was told

later that not only were these the living quarters of the locals but also the living accommodation for their cattle and livestock.

As we got off the aircraft we said our goodbyes to the crew. I gave Maureen a kiss – or rather, she gave me a hug and a kiss. We said we should have to meet again sometime. Ironically, I have never seen her from that day onwards, and very often wonder what became of her.

As I came out of the fuselage onto the steps to go down onto the tarmac I thought to myself, hell, those engines are warm, I can feel the heat radiating from here. As I went down the steps the heat from the engines didn't seem to subside. It wasn't until I had walked about a hundred yards away from the aircraft, that I realised that the heat was not from the engines, but the heat from the setting sun. It was an entirely different heat to any I had ever experienced before. It was a very dry heat, almost like one would get from an electric fire at home.

We walked towards the terminal, which was painted white, but had a few cracks in the masonry, due to the lack of maintenance. One of the passengers walking beside me remarked how it had rather deteriorated in appearance since he had been there during the war. We walked into the terminal, up a slope, turned right onto a platform and right across a room that was dark and filled with smoke. I could hear some moaning from afar to the right of us. It wasn't until I was halfway across the room that I realised that we were all walking across a stage where a film show was in progress and we were walking right in front of the screen, causing a shadow of ourselves on it, and blocking the bottom part of the film that was in progress.

We were escorted into a waiting room, and handed a glass of fruit juice as we entered. The heat was unbearable, and although we were in a room with the fans above us circulating the air, the air was still stifling. I found that I really wanted to take off some of the clothing that I wore. For the first time I could see myself as a mad, mad Englishman out in the midday sun. The only difference was that it was now six thirty in the evening, and I was perspiring more than I had ever done in my whole life. It was daft. Here was I, in Bombay, and still with my bloody vest, shirt, tie, and pullover on. I had to do something about this. It was unbearable. I looked around for the gents' toilets, so that I could get some of my clothing off. As I was about to enter the gents', I thought to myself. Now don't be mad, Baker. In a matter of an hour or so you will be off again, making for Singapore. According to the airline captain, we're suppose to land at Singapore (Paya Lebar)

Airport at around six in the morning. Don't go getting undressed too much. It may be cold in Singapore at that time of morning. You don't want to catch a cold through not having enough clothing on.

In the gents' toilets I found a mirror and decided that all I was going to take off was my tie and pullover. After all, if it got cold at Singapore, I could just put my tie and pullover on again. I took my tie off first, rolled it up and put into my bag. I then proceeded to take off my pullover. As I was half in and half out of my pullover, Alf came in. 'Oh there you are; thought you might have been with Maureen for the last few minutes. You crafty old bugger, you. You certainly kept a low profile when it came to her.'

I tried to change the subject straight away. 'No. I said my goodbyes on the aircraft. Anyway, she's gone now. But it was nice to see her again after all this time.'

Alf jumped onto my last comment straight away. 'What! Well, you crafty old bastard, you. She was one of your old floozies all the time! Here was I thinking that you didn't know her, and it was the first time you had met her.'

Whilst Alf was going on about Maureen, I had folded my pullover up and put it into my bag along with my tie. I proceeded over to a sink unit and started to put some cold water into it. Alf just carried on getting more jealous by the minute. I thought to myself, carry on our kid. You're going to blow a fuse in a minute. But you still ain't going to know anything about her. I'll let you carry on, and think what you want to think.

I proceeded to swill my face and hands, which made me feel a lot better than I had since coming off the aircraft. I wiped my face and hands with a paper towel. Alf was still carrying on. 'Alright Alf, so I made it with an air hostess. So what? I still ain't going to tell you anything about her. So you might as well shut up and let it be.' Alf just stood there completely dumbfounded, with his mouth wide open. 'Come on Alf, let's go and get another drink. It's still too bloody hot in here,' I said as I picked up my bag and proceeded towards the exit door. Alf followed like a lost sheep. 'I can't get over you, Mike,' Alf started as we came out the door of the gents.

'What can't you get over?' I asked. 'You! Your attitude towards women is completely different to what I thought it would be.'

'Look!' I said, as I turned to him. 'I made it with an air hostess. OK, so what? Now that's the end of it. It's over. forget it. I knew her from years ago and that's all there is to it. So let's go and get a drink and forget the whole thing. I'm getting a little fed up of hearing you go on about Maureen. Think what you like about her. But for goodness sake keep it to yourself,' I admonished him. 'Do I make myself clear?' I asked. Alf looked at me in complete disbelief.

'Yeah I hear you,' and with that he changed the subject. 'OK so what are we going to have to drink?' he asked. By now we had reached the bar.

'All I want is a nice cool Coke, please,' I replied.

The Britannia took off again for the last part of our journey. We had been informed that the flight would be an all-night one, flying over India across the Bay of Bengal, down over the Andaman Sea, and finally following down the west coast of Malaya to land at Singapore's Payar Lebar Airport at six in the morning. We were settled down for the night flight, after being given supper. Blankets, earplugs and eye masks were issued as they had been for the first part of our flight between Stansted and Yesilkoy. I tried to settle down to sleep, but knew in my heart that I would never be able to, so I tried to lie on my side, so that, although I was covered up with the blanket, I was still able to look out of the window, daft as it may seem, since I wasn't going to be able to see anything, especially as most of the flight was going to be over the sea.

After about an hour of flight the cabin lights were put out so everyone could get some shut-eye. The aircraft was in semi-darkness, as it droned on and on through the night. I for my part just looked out of the window, looking at nothing. As time went by the droning of the engines, and my looking out at nothing, had an effect and I gradually dozed off to sleep.

Next morning, Alf woke me up, complaining that I had gone off to sleep so deeply that I had snored so loudly and kept most of the other passenger awake for most of the night. I replied that I didn't believe him and that he was kidding me.

Approximately an hour before the flight was due to land the captain's voice came over the Tannoy to say that we would be landing in approximately an hour's time. The temperature at Singapore was ninety degrees Fahrenheit, with the humidity being very high at eighty. On hearing this, I decided that I wouldn't put my tie or pullover back on . . .

At exactly six the Britannia touched down at Singapore Airport. The aircraft taxied to the terminal and stopped just away from a large building. We collected our belongings from the compartment above our seats and began to disembark from the plane. As I came out of the fuselage of the aircraft the heat hit me with so much force that it was like being slapped in the face with a hot flannel. As Alf and I were going down the steps from the aircraft Alf looked up to me and said. 'Cor, what in heaven is that taste and smell?'

The atmosphere was very close, and extremely humid, although it was still early in the morning. There was that strong smell, and a taste of dead vegetation starting to form on our lips, as Alf had mentioned. By the time I had reached the bottom of the steps of the aircraft the humidity had started to make my forehead perspire. My vest and shirt started to become wet and in turn clung to my body. The perspiration was different from home. Whereas at home the perspiration would run down your face and back, here it was inclined to cling to you in globules.

All around the airfield, you could hear croaking and high pitched whistling.

We walked to the immigration lounge where we had our passports inspected. We were asked which of the services we were in, Army, Navy or Air force. How did they know by our passports that we were in the services. As I was naïve, it took me ages to find out. When they found out which service we were in we were ushered into a separate room, away from all the other civilian passengers that were on our flight.

After a few minutes of waiting, an RAF Officer came into the room and called out our last three numbers, rank and name. After each reply, he would announce which coach we were to proceed to – coach number one, two or three. I had to go onto coach number one. I was on my own, as Alf had to go to Seletar Base. I went outside the terminal building to get onto the coach. It was still very hot, sticky and humid. It was once again an atmosphere that I had never experienced before. I still had that horrible taste of dead vegetation on my lips. I could also feel the stickiness getting to my body. In fact my vest was already sticking to my back. It was most uncomfortable. All around me appeared to be nothing else but trees. From the trees one could hear rustling, and strange noise. There was the odd building here and there. As I walked towards the coach, I saw very large beetle-like insects running around on the ground. I stepped onto the coach, only to find that these beetles were crawling around the coach floor. They varied between half an inch to about an inch in size, and were yellowed brown in colour. As the driver of the coach got on, he stepped on one of these beetles. With a loud crack, the beetle was crushed under his foot. The driver's comment was 'bloody cockroaches, they get everywhere. If you lads see them, KILL the bloody things. They're a bleeding menace.'

'What in the hell have I let myself in for with this horrible place,' I thought to myself. Everything seemed so different from the tropical paradise I had been told about, and been eagerly expecting.

Chapter Nine

RAF Changi

BY THE TIME the coach had started to roll it was approximately seven in the morning. It was still dark, but there was a hint of dawn breaking. Suddenly, within a minute or so, it became a bright sunny morning, just as if someone had turned an electric light on the world. The coach travelled for about half an hour. When on the right of the road appeared a long runway. Then around two hundred yards on, as we appeared to be going up a slope, the coach seemed to go past the main gateway of RAF Changi on the left. All this could be seen as it was now light. We were taken down the main road. But instead of going into an RAF camp, the coach came to, and went through, a village.

The village appeared to have a tarmac single-lane road for traffic, and just enough room for two cars or lorries to pass. On each side of the road was a wide dusty verge, approximately twenty to thirty feet in width, with the odd car parked here and there. The back of the verge and on each side of the village was a line of large trees, with a wide canopy of foliage, which intermittently caused an archway over the road. Behind the trees one could see rows of old shacks. These were shops of all descriptions, from tailors, to photography. Each shop looked as if it was made from old wood and the roofs were formed from corrugated sheeting. Above the shops were signs written in Chinese, and English. Along the whole length of the shops on both sides were long covered walk ways for shoppers to stay under if it rained, or to keep them out of the hot sun. At one place on the right, I noticed a couple of people in khaki uniforms, seated at a table drinking. I found out later that they were Airmen at Fred's Café. There was something about this village which I liked. Although I was passing through it, I could feel it had a character, and an atmosphere. The village was called Changi village. Before long, I was to spend many happy days there.

At the end of the village the coach turned right into a gateway, and moved towards a medium sized building. This was where the passengers who had brought their families out with them were to alight. They were escorted by Chinese personnel into the families' transit block. The building was quite impressive. It was made of wood, but looked more like a hotel. The approach road to the building was crescent-shaped so that you went in by one entrance, and came out by another. It was lined with tropical plants, and medium fan-like palm trees.

After the married personnel had disembarked at the transit block the coach took the rest of the passengers, who were single, to another transit block where we were to stay until we had been given our permanent place of residence. We arrived there by going around, what seemed at the time like a maze of roads. We eventually stopped outside a light green concrete building which had a wide open archway with a stone staircase leading up to an additional two floors. The building had a wide covered veranda all around the perimeter and on each floor. On the outside of the veranda on the ground floor was a drain about a foot deep and set back inside the veranda were louvre windows, and doors leading into the billet.

The remainder of the passengers on the coach were told to get off, and to find a pit for themselves. We were informed that we would be given twenty four hours to rest and to recuperate from our travels. We were to be ready next day for our initiation at RAF Changi. In other words we were to find our own way around the camp.

I still couldn't get used to the horrible smell and taste of dead vegetation on my lips, but I couldn't do much about it anyway, except to wipe my mouth with the back of my hand every now and then. It was approximately 08.00 hours by now. We were all very tired, and more or less followed one another like sheep up to the top floor. Why the top floor? That I just don't know. As we got there all we could see was a room full of beds in rows. There were a few other erks inside who had possibly arrived the day before. None of the lads who arrived with me asked them as we were all too tired. Each bed that was empty was equipped with a mattress, a pillow and two white cotton sheets with the bed already made. We each selected a pit, and collapsed onto our beds, going off to sleep more or less straight away. Some of the lads undressed down to their underclothes. Some of the others stripped completely.

I awoke some hours later with quite a start. As I opened my eyes, I saw that above me, crawling across the ceiling, was a lizard. It was a greenish-yellow colour, and about four inches long. I jumped out of bed, not really looking where I was, and still looking up at this lizard. In the background, I could hear a burst of laughter. Another erk, who must have been there a little longer than myself, laughingly said, 'Don't worry about them, mate, they're Chit-Chats (geckos). It's just as well we have them around, as they eat a lot of mossies (mosquitos). You'll find loads of Chit-Chats everywhere. If you catch one and hold it by its tail, it'll release its tail, and leave you with a tail wiggling in your fingers.'

'Who are you?' I asked him, thanking him at the same time for the information.

'I'm here to help you find your bearings mate,' he replied.

By now a few of the others had woken up. It looked as if most of them had slept well, as, at first, none of them seemed to know where they were.

Another inmate enquired as to where he could cool down and have a bath, as he was (as all of us were) feeling really hot and especially sticky.

'You'll have to get used to this heat and humidity. It's like this all the year round out here, day and night. In this country you have one season, and that is summer, summer, summer, and summer,' the man emphasised. 'You'll be wanting to have a shower very often, and be spending most of your time off duty at the swimming pool,' our new leader continued. I had the impression that he meant every word he spoke.

'The showers are out there,' he added, pointing at the same time.

I followed his finger and went to the out-house that our new leader had indicated, with just a towel around my waist. The floors of the building had no linoleum or mats. Just plain smooth concrete floors, but to the bare feet, the floor was warm and I didn't mind. 'If only I can get rid of this horrible taste in my mouth,' I thought.

The out-house where the showers were, appeared to be away from the building as such, and had to be reached by walking across the veranda, or bridge. As I walked across it to reach the showers, I noticed a wood across the road from the block. Some of the trees appeared to be banana trees and some were large broad trees with a sort of fern-like leaf on them, with large black dried pods about twelve to eighteen inches long hanging from the branches. If you can imagine a large runner bean that had dried up, that was what these pods looked like. I came to find out later that this tree was commonly known as 'The Flame of the Jungle' and also why it was called this. In the background one could hear the sound of crickets, and other croaking sounds, as if from frogs. Every now and then there were screaming and whistling noises. The noises were just as I had heard in films which had been set in the tropics. I began to wonder if I was in paradise.

I went into have my first shower, which, to be honest, was one of the most pleasant cool showers I remember having in my entire stay in Singapore. I dried myself off and proceeded to clean my teeth in the sink opposite the shower, partly hoping that I might be able to get rid of this taste in my mouth. The cold water from the tap was not at all cold, but had a cool warmth all of its own. It's hard to describe.

I looked out over the veranda to see, swinging in the trees quite close to me, three or four monkeys. They seemed to be so free, and happy. It was at this point, whilst watching these monkeys, that it sank in. I really was in a tropical country. I wasn't dreaming. The atmosphere being given off around the whole area made me feel that the following year or so was to be possibly the happiest period of my life. The screaming and the swinging of those monkeys seemed to be an omen to me.

After having that wonderful cool shower I dried myself off. Our new guide saw me wiping my ears. 'Make sure that you clean and dry your ears out here, my old mate.'

'What makes you say that, or are you taking the rise, or something?' I asked, indignantly.

My guide laughed. 'No!' as he put his arms up high in surrender. 'No, if you don't keep your ears clean and especially dry, the dampness in your ears can become fungused. If that happens you'll know all about it,' he explained.

Whilst making sure that my ears were properly dry, I looked out over the veranda to see what was surrounding the billet. The billet appeared to be set on the side of a hill. Below me, I could see a large playing field and beyond that I could see traffic going up and down a road. The whole surroundings appeared to be such a lush green. The atmosphere was so magical. There didn't seem to be any cause for rushing around. Not like back in England, where everything seemed to be needed to be done yesterday.

In the background to my left I could hear a lot of screaming, like a group of schoolchildren out playing. I walked around the veranda towards where the noises were coming from. To my surprise, just across the road was a large school, and the children were on their afternoon break in the playground.

Our leader, or guide, told us where the mess was to be found, so that the group that had come with me in the coach could get something to eat and drink. As we entered the mess, the other Airmen turned to see who had arrived, then turned back to whatever they were doing, but with snide grins on their faces.

Next day, we were up and dressed in our new khaki tropical uniforms. Our knees were as white as snow. We all felt ill at ease, and very conspicuous, especially after our guide started to take the mickey out of us.

'You lot look like you've just come out from Blighty. A right lot of moonies you are,' he chuckled. 'Never mind, you'll soon learn!'

The reason we all felt ill at ease, was because the shorts that we were wearing looked more like something from another age, where everyone else we had seen in tropical uniform looked smart. Their uniforms looked as if they had been made from another kind of material. Even the few officers we had seen were the same. The shorts especially, were a lot shorter than ours. The ones we had been issued with came down to or below our knees where everyone else's came down to approximately four to six inches above the knee.

Our guide informed us that he was not coming around with us, due to the fact that each one of us had a different trade, which meant that we would all be going to different parts of the camp during the day. Also, we would not necessarily be in the same billet. He pointed to a building across the playing field.

'That is the main admin block. You all go there first, to see the Admin Officer. He will give you different forms to be taken to different parts of the camp so that you'll be signed in.'

As we walked along the road in a group towards the Admin Section we all kept getting wolf whistles from some of the camp personnel, especially as RAF vehicles went past. Everyone seemed to like taking the piss out of us. Some would shout as they passed 'What-ho moonies!' We really did get the treatment. All we could do was to grin and bear it, and to join in the fun by waving back at the vehicles as they passed.

Once we had arrived at the Admin Block even there, a kind of smirk seemed to linger on people's faces. The Admin Officer's Assistants gave us the forms, and a map of the camp, plus a few booklets on Singapore, etc. We were then told where we had to report first. I was unfortunate – that I had to walk around the camp on my own, due to the fact that I was the only teleprinter operator. We were told that the walk around the camp would take the rest of the day. I was told in which direction to start walking and then to use my own initiative to find my way around the camp. I came out of the Admin Block on to the road I could see from the Transit Block. It was the same road that I had gone down the day before in the coach. I had to go up the road, but as I looked down it I could see Changi village not more than two hundred yards away. I started to walk up the road to where I was eventually to find the place I was to work. That was the communication centre (Com-cen) Changi.

Com-cen Changi was off the main Road (Upper Changi Road) and to the right (Churchdown Road) beside the main runway of the airfield. The airfield itself looked massive. I could just make out the coastline in the distance by a row of palm trees on the other side of the airfield. I signed on at Com-cen Changi and I was told my permanent billet was to be block 144, and that all wireless ops and teleprinter ops were billeted on the very top floor. I was also informed my pay was to be eighty-four (Singapore) dollars a fortnight, and I was expected to be on pay parade every other Wednesday at 11.00 hours, here at the back of the Com-cen. There was at that time eight dollars fifty-four to one pound which worked out, with overseas allowance, to be nine pounds eighty-four pence a fortnight. This was all a National Serviceman was entitled to.

I was to report for duty the following morning at 08.00 hours. My hours of duty were to be: 08.00 – 13.00, 18.00 – 23.59 (Mdt), 13.00 – 18.00 hours, 23.59 – 08.00 hours next morning.

I would then have the rest of the day off, plus the following day, and had to report back at 08.00 the following day, which meant I would be off duty for a whole forty-eight hours.

I was then instructed to go to the guardroom. To get there, I had to go back onto the Main Road, and walk about a hundred yards, and then turn right into Tangmere Road. As I turned into Tangmere Road, there was the main gate that I had passed, when arriving by coach, not more than twenty-four hours earlier. I had to go past a barrier which stretched across the road, and walk up a flight of steps into the guardroom on the left. As I entered, I was met by an RAF policeman calling out to someone else inside, 'We got another moonie arriving.'

'Oh no! Not another one,' came the reply.

Also from an RAF policeman, who was grinning from ear to ear. 'You musn't take too much notice of these comments, my old mate. It's the usual greeting from all the erks in the camp when they see a new erk arriving,' he said to me.

'Thanks. That makes feel a lot better,' I replied. I was already feeling very conspicuous, and comments of this nature didn't exactly reassure me.

'Even if you were as black as the ace of spades we can pick you out,' he added.

'Oh! how's that?' I asked.

A voice came from the back of the guardroom. 'Because of your Bermuda shorts, and your lily-white legs, moonie,' Everyone in the room started to laugh.

'As I said, all the moonies get the same treatment when they get here on their first day walk about,' he was grinning as before. 'You'll be doing the same thing yourself in a few months' time. It's all part of the initiation here in Changi.'

After he had dealt with all the documentation I asked him where I had to go from there.

'You have to go to see the MO which is just around the corner from here in Old Sarum Road, more or less at the back of here,' the Corporal said. 'In that yellow book you have in your hand you'll find, in the middle pages, a map of the camp. If you think the walk is getting too long, you can always catch a bus.'

I went on my way. As I came down the steps of the guardroom, I was once again met by a lot wolf-whistles and jeers from a lorry full of Airmen in the back. I returned the gesture with a 'V' sign. I was now getting really pissed off with it, but what could I do. From the guardroom, I went on to the MO, and then to find out where my

permanent place of residence was. Fortunately, I was told by the MO
that block 144 was in Martlesham Road, and only just around the
corner, opposite the fire brigade's billets. Also it was not far from the
Sergeants Mess.

I found block 144 with little trouble. The block was similar to the
transit block, but a lot longer and it was painted white. I climbed the
stairs to the top floor, as I had been instructed by Com-cen Changi.
As I was climbing the stairs, one or two erks were coming down. As
they passed I got the usual look, and one of them remarked in a kind
of greeting 'Hi! Moonie,' I asked them if there were empty pits on the
floor and their reply was to pick any one that did not have sheets on.

Whilst I walked along the long veranda I was greeted by the other
inhabitants with a whistling rendition of the Laurel and Hardy theme
tune. 'De-de-de De-de-de Diddly-de Diddly-de De-de-de De-de-de
Diddly-de Da de-de,' and so on. I felt a right fool.

As I was walking I looked in through the door of each room to see
if there were any spare beds. The billet floor consisted of seven rooms.
The middle room looked as if it was a recreational room and on each
side of this were three rooms with about ten beds in them.

One of the erks who was lying on his pit reading a magazine looked
up and said in a real Welsh twang, ' Hi Moonie. Where are you
working? My name's Taffy Morgan.'

'Hi!' I replied. ' I'm Mike Baker. I'm looking for somewhere to
perch in this billet.' Then added 'I'm suppose to be working in Com-
cen Changi. They instructed me to come to this billet.'

Taffy Morgan swung himself out of his pit, came over to me, and
offered his hand in welcome. 'That's right. All of us on this floor work
in Com-cen Changi, or work on communications of some sort. Put
your stuff over there on that pit.' He pointed to an empty bed. 'I'll get
the bearer to make up your bed.'

'The bearer?' I asked confused.

'Yeah! That's right,' Taff answered. 'You don't do anything here
that's not to do with your work at Com-cen Changi,' he added.

I looked at him, even more confused.

He laughed. 'It's alright,' he said. 'We all pay two Singapore dollars
a fortnight. For that, the bearer cleans the room, makes your bed, and
is generally your servant.' Taff was still laughing at my mystification.
'He's also a money lender. That comes in handy towards the end of
the week, when you get a bit skint.'

'Servant!' I looked at him in disbelief.

'You're not in Blighty now, you know,' he stated. 'Your life will be entirely different to back home. This is known as a holiday camp throughout the RAF,' Taff informed me.

I could now understand the Officer back at RAF Compton Bassett commenting that I was one of the luckiest fellows.

By now there were a few more erks coming into the room. They were all wearing nothing more than a towel around their waists, or just a pair of underpants. Some were wet, as if they had just come out of the showers. Taffy was in the same state of dress. I could well understand the mode of dress, as it was by now exceptionally hot. I guessed that it must have been approximately a hundred degrees Fahrenheit. At least to me it seemed like it.

'He's right, you know.' One of the newcomers said to Taff's comment and then went on to introduce himself. 'Hi! I'm Steve Callaghan. I work in the Com-cen as well. I'm a wireless op,' and then enquiring, 'and what trade are you?'

'Me? I'm suppose to be a teleprinter operator,' I said sheepishly.

Then another fellow who stood by the door introduced himself. 'Come on. The first thing we have to do with you is get you kitted out properly, and out of those godforsaken clothes.' He stuck out his hand suddenly. 'Hi! I'm sorry mate. I should have said. I'm Geordie Hoskins.'

And I'm so and so. They all started to introduce themselves. Each shaking my hand in turn.

While all this was going on Taff had gone to get the bearer who had brought with him clean bed sheets and pillows and suchlike, and had started to make up my bed. He was of Indian or Pakistani extraction, and middle aged. He was wearing a short kind of sarong that came down to just above his knees. Also, he wore an old chequered shirt. On his feet he wore a pair of well worn flip-flops made of rubber. I had noticed that no matter where I had been around the camp everyone not in uniform was wearing these flip-flops.

I noticed now that while I was getting myself settled in by unpacking my things each one of the erks seemed to be interested in various aspects of what was happening at home in Britain. What was the weather like? What was the latest in politics, or what scandals were there, etc.

By the time I had unpacked, and been taken back to the transit block to pick up my other belongings, it was getting on for three o'clock in the afternoon. For some unknown reason, one of the first things that I observed about my new surroundings was that just outside of my room, on the veranda, I could see that a leaning rail along the outside edge was missing. The veranda itself was approximately six feet in width and surrounded the complete block. Also, in each room were two fans, suspended from the high ceiling. They were a godsend to me for the first few weeks I was out there.

Rather than be the laughing-stock for the rest of the camp, my new work-mates had persuaded me to change into some other civilian clothes. If I didn't have the required clothing then it was loaned to me for the time being. This was so they could take me around the camp, and down to the village to get a new made-to-measure uniform. I was told my uniform would be ready by the evening. As well as getting some other types of civilian clothing, which were more in keeping with the new climate I had to get acclimatised to, I was feeling a lot more comfortable in myself once I had my new uniform. I felt as if I were being steered in the right direction.

Whilst being taken around the camp by my new companion I found out exactly how large RAF Changi was. It was so big that Changi village was situated in one corner of the camp, and there was a bus service around the camp every thirty minutes. The airfield took up approximately half of the camp, and the whole of the area, the complete east corner of Singapore Island. The camp, although under military rule, was an easy-going place. Provided you did what was expected, you were left to enjoy life. There was a distinct atmosphere here and I was to find out as time went by that the easy-going ambience was due partly to its infamous past. There was always an air of happiness, but also a reverence for the past.

Changi had several different air forces under its wing. There was of course the Royal Air Force, but also the Royal Malayan Air Force, the Royal Australian Air Force, and the Royal New Zealand Air Force. The RAF had three Squadrons. Nos 48, with Hastings aircraft, and 205 Squadron with MR2 Shackleton reconnaissance aircraft. Plus three aircraft belonging to the Far East Communication Squadron. The RAAF had a Squadron of Bristol freighter cargo aircraft, and so did the RNZAF. Apart from the above. There was a small Army detachment of Royal Signals, a small detachment of Forty-second Commando, Royal Marines, Queen Alexandra's Nursing Service, who staffed the Changi hospital and many others.

The main places for rest and relaxation were the Malcolm Club, opposite the NAAFI, which fortunately for me was only about a hundred yards down Martlesham Road. Across the road from the Malcolm Club in Tangmere Road was the Astra cinema. There was the swimming pool, right opposite the hospital, not far from the village. As for the evening, the best place was down in Changi village. During our days off, of course, there was Singapore City, which was approximately twenty miles away and could be reached by bus or taxi. I was told all this as the days went by, by my new comrades.

A couple of days after I had started work at Com-cen Changi, I was instructed to go to the Astra cinema at 10.30 a.m. to watch some films that would be of educational value to me. If I happened to be on duty, then I would be allowed time off so that I would not miss this series of films. I was then to learn something that would live with me, and would never forget.

I went to the Malcolm Club first at around 09.30 hours, along with some of my new friends from the block, to have a drink or two. I had told them earlier, that I had to see some educational films of some sort or other. The only replies I got was that they were very educational, and that the films would never be forgotten. From what I was told, everyone that came to Changi would see these films within a few days of arrival.

At 10.15 hours I made my way to the cinema. I noticed that there were quite a few WRAF personnel as well as other erks. I should imagine there were approximately fifty to sixty persons there altogether. All of them had only arrived in Singapore not more than a couple of weeks ago. We all sat down in the cinema. Everyone was talking about these films that were to be shown. There was a whisper that they were of a tourist nature but no one knew exactly.

Once everyone was inside the cinema, and seated, a Medical Officer came down the aisle, between the seats, and onto the stage.

'Good morning everyone,' he started. Everyone nodded, and mumbled a 'good morning' back.

'Right, ladies and gentlemen. I expect you have wondered what this is all about. I expect some of you have heard about what you're about to see.' He looked around the audience, to see what the response was. 'The films that you are about to see are of grave importance to your personal safety and well being. I hope for your sakes that

none of you are squeamish, because these films are about venereal
diseases. Especially gonorrhoea and syphilis. They apply to both sexes,
and that's why you are all here today. Whether you like these films or
not, you will watch them because they could save you a lot of
discomfort, pain and embarrassment.' He paused to let his words sink
in to everyone in the cinema. Then he started again. 'Some of the
scenes are very gruesome, and are meant to be so that they will put
some of you off going to visit the local ladies of this country.' He then
looked up, and around towards the WRAFs who were amongst the
audience. 'The reason some of you ladies are here is to let you see
what the effects can be on yourselves as well, should you contract one
of these diseases. Believe me, you can become affected. You only have
to be involved with an Airman, or anybody for that matter, who has
been with other women, and who has one of these diseases, and even
though he or she may not know that they have caught the clap, they
can just as easily pass it on to you.'

He stopped once more, to let things sink in again. 'Finally, let there
be no mistake. If any one of you gets venereal disease, or thinks that
he or she may have it, then go to the MO and get treatment for it,
straight away. Failing to do so can be construed, like sunburn, as a self-
inflicted wound, which can be a Court Martial offence.' He was
looking all around the auditorium.

'Right, lights out. Cameraman, let the films begin,' he ordered.

The lights went out, and the films started to roll.

I had never seen a blue movie, let alone a film on venereal diseases
before. So, to a certain extent, I was a little uncomfortable about seeing these films. As they were in colour and very graphic, my stomach
got more and more queasy. I could hear behind as well as in front of
me, different comments being passed. The films gave close-up views
of the different stages of gonorrhoea and syphilis. Both on men, as
well as women. It was enough to make you want to be ill. They truly
were sickening films. I'm sure some of the audience had to run out to
the toilets to be sick. If that was meant to be the objective of the films
– to make you ill – then they certainly were very effective. Every now
and then, especially when a close-up came onto the screen of one disease or the other, several of the audience gave out a loud, 'U-u-ugh'.
The screen showed both male and female parts of the anatomy, and
how distorted and inflamed these could be when diseased.

As for myself, I found them very, very gruesome, and I vowed to myself that I wouldn't touch a prostitute while I was in Singapore. I'm sure I, as well as many others, came out of the cinema feeling quite sick, and white in the face.

After being in camp for a little while, you would come to know some of the local characters. One was a woman by the name of Mary Tan OBE. Her story deserves telling, and re-telling for it is a tale of human courage, and fortitude, of the suffering and misery which was borne by a very, very brave woman.

Mary's early married life gave no hint of the tragedy that was to come; she settled down happily with her husband and by the age of twenty-nine, in 1942, she was a mother of three sons and three daughters.

The Tans were a close-knit family in the best Chinese tradition. Their horizons were bright and the start of the Japanese war troubled them little. Was not Singapore a great fortress, proof against any invader?

But the Japanese invaded in February 1942, and quickly Mary's happiness was in ruins. She was forced to watch her husband brutally murdered while she stood by helplessly. From then until the liberation in 1945 she worked ceaselessly for the Allied cause in Singapore.

In Changi prison camp were many thousands of Allied POWs. To these men Mary smuggled food, drink, and cigarettes for over three years, braving the Japanese guards each time. To the POWs she was an angel of mercy, and the food she brought meant the difference between life and death to many of them. She has appeared in many books written by former POWs and after the war her courage was recognised by the award of the OBE. Mary Tan was very proud of her decoration and of the privilege that the Royal Air Force granted her in honour of her work – permission to go, unrestricted, around RAF Changi and sell fruit to Officers and alike.

Whilst I was there, she must have been approximately forty-eight years of age. Mary had picked up the threads of her life, and you would find her pushing her diminutive cart around the barrack blocks or carrying huge loads of fruit in her baskets. She was a cheerful generous person who loved to joke. To hungry Airmen she was once again the angel of mercy for she never refused a plea for 'Just a couple of apples until pay day, Mary.' Her English vocabulary included many phrases not normally used in the drawing room. Sometimes she would swear like a trooper, and make the Airmen go red with embarrassment. Her quaint mixture of Malay, English, Hindustani and Chinese caused many a chuckle. A sincere Christian, Mary, after a day's hard work selling fruit, would go home at night to her family in Changi village where she lived in a small house.

One story about Mary Tan that has been told many times was of the day she was found lying in the road near Changi village with her fruit scattered all over the place. She had been knocked down by a taxi and it was at first feared that she had been seriously hurt. But needless to say, she was not. Within five minutes she was exchanging 'blue' jokes in Malay with the policeman who had been sent to the scene of her accident! A little later, having gathered her fruit, she was off with a cheerful wave to the nearest barrack block to sing out 'Hey Johnny, you want to buy . . .'

To Airmen looking back on their tour, as I often do, Mary was part of Changi; a legend in her own time; and many took photographs of her with her baskets of fruit to show folks at home. I, for one kept an article in *RAF Changi Magazine* about her, parts of which I have used to tell this tale.

Chapter Ten

Changi Murals

BELOW MY BILLET (block 144,) was block 151. In this block I once saw something that will stay in my memory for the rest of my living days. On the ground floor in the corner was an empty room which have some famous paintings. They are known as the 'Changi Murals'. The following is a record of those murals and how they came about.

Wartime captivity in Changi was, to put it mildly, among the most degrading of human experiences, but from such experiences there come stories of courage and faith.

The suffering of Bombardier Stanley Warren is such a story.

During the Japanese occupation, block 151 was the dysentery wing of a hospital, staffed by medical personnel of the RAMC field ambulance units 196, 197 and 198.

While the doctors tended the sick bodies of the wounded, the Reverend F H Stallard ministered to their spiritual needs. No mean task under such grim circumstances, but the Reverend Stallard managed to obtain permission from the grudging Japanese commander to convert part of the ground floor into a chapel. With the aid of the prisoners, and under the supervision of an officer of the 18th Division, the interior was decorated in the style befitting a chapel, and a dedication ceremony conferred the name of St Luke's chapel upon the grim surroundings. It was into block 151, and into these surroundings, that soldiers of the 135th Field Regiment were brought, suffering from serious wounds.

One of these soldiers was Bombardier Stanley Warren.

No drugs or medical aids were available, but the staff, after many weeks of careful nursing, managed to pull him through the crisis.

Stanley, a very religious man, was grateful to God for giving him life when so many were being denied it. He was inspired, and decided to decorate the walls of the chapel with murals as his thanksgiving to God for his recovery. He painted five murals in all, and St Luke's chapel really began to look a house of worship. Toc H held regular meetings there and, at one time, a magazine was produced by the prisoners for distribution in the hospital wards.

The years passed and with the Japanese occupation ended, the chapel was deserted. The murals were forgotten until 1958 when *Tale-Spin* (RAF Changi's local magazine) published pictures of them, saying that all efforts to trace the artist had failed.

Then the hunt began.

A young lady from Singapore started the ball rolling by sending a letter to the *Daily Mirror,* asking the 'old codgers' to find the unknown artist. The *Mirror* reproduced one of the pictures from *Tale-Spin,* and this immediately sparked off a nation-wide interest. Letters were received, and published, giving various accounts of how the murals came to be painted.

The Singapore *Sunday Times* took up the search and contacted ex-POWs who had been interned at Changi during the war.

The most popular suggestion was that the murals were done by Ronald Searle, the famous artist and cartoonist, but when he was approached in London he said that the paintings he had done in Changi Jail were twelve feet high, while those in block 151 were not nearly so big. Further searching revealed another two murals in the map store in block 34, but these also were much bigger than those in block 151. While the search was continuing the answer was finally discovered, curiously enough, in Changi itself.

A book came to light in the FEAF (Far East Air Force) educational library which gave the answer to the mystery, and the story of Bombardier Stanley Warren was revealed. The book, entitled *Churches of the Captivity in Malaya,* had solved the mystery of the painter's name, but the artist himself had not been found.

Meanwhile, Vincent Ng of the *Sunday Times* had contacted a Mr Philip J Weyer of Nationale Handelsbank in Singapore, who had been in the same ward as the artist. He remembered Stanley as a very quiet man, religious by nature, who insisted that his murals were a gift to God, and that he refused to sign his work, though his friends tried hard to persuade him to do so. Inevitably, it lay with the *Daily Mirror,* with its circulation of millions, to find the shy artist of Changi. Early in February 1959, the search came to an end when Stanley Warren was discovered in his present occupation as arts master at Sir William Collins Secondary School in North London, where he lived with his wife and one son. He was surprised by the interest that his murals had stirred in England and Singapore, considering that they were then fourteen years old. He said that he never regarded them as great works of art, since he was greatly hampered by a lack of materials. He had used dark brown decorating paint for oils, and made brushes with scraps of material that came to hand, and admitted that he never thought that his crude attempts would be remembered.

Today (September 1961) block 151 is undergoing structural changes, and new partition walls are being built inside. Due to an unfortunate accident which took place during this redecoration, the murals were damaged. An attempt has been made to patch them up, but the ravages of time have already had a deleterious affect upon the paint; it is fading and crumbling. It would be a great pity if they were allowed to rot into obscurity. They were more than just paintings; more than just figures on a wall. They are the living proof of the unconquerable human spirit; the symbolic representation of a man's soul crying out in anguish, seeking, searching for some way to thank his God for giving him life and hope. There is no reason why the murals should be preserved. To paint them again with new paints would detract something from their intrinsic, and spiritual, value, but perhaps they could be preserved in their present condition by spraying the wall with a light varnish.

Today, (1961) only three of the original murals remain, side by side on one wall, and the middle mural contains the greatest words of all time:

'Father, forgive them, for they know not what they do.'

The above story is copied from RAF Changi's magazine, *Tale-Spin* September 1961 issue. I admit this is not my story, but I found that the way it is told is far better than I could ever tell it.

The murals when I saw them were as the story says, very worn, and fading. Damage had been done to one mural. It had a hole knocked through it so that a door could be put into the wall. After someone had realised what damage had been done, the hole in the wall had been rebuilt and re-plastered. Unfortunately, nothing could be done about the mural. There was also a myth growing around the camp that nothing could destroy the murals. No matter what destruction or mutilation was done to them, the murals would come back again to their original state.

The mural that I found to be so appropriate and most sacred was the painting of the Christ being hoisted up, pinned to the cross, with the words as said in the report, 'Father, forgive them –' to be so very, very fitting. It always gave me a lump in my the throat when I looked at it.

Chapter Eleven

Changi Village

CHANGI WAS A village of history, of infamy, but at the same time, it had a charm all of its own. There were villagers who had been in the brutal hands of the Japanese, during the occupation – I mentioned Mary Tan earlier, as an example. I'm sure there were others whose stories have never been told.

I found that the villagers were very trusting. Those that owned shops would sometimes let you have goods on the knock, especially once they got to know you. In other words, they would let you have the goods you required, and you could pay for them on pay day. Customer and vendor – each respected the other. There were, of course, the odd one or two disputes, but on the whole, it was a good working relationship amongst the servicemen and the shopkeepers.

Changi village was situated at the very eastern end of the island of Singapore. It was also completely surrounded by RAF Changi. On one side, there were the billets, and on the other side was the airfield. To get to Changi hospital direct, and the Pagar (playing field) and further on to HQFEAF (Headquarters, Far East Air Force) one would have to go through the village. Although there were other routes, they took a more roundabout way. The only route to and from the village, and Singapore City was by the main Upper Changi Road, which followed a line between the billets and the airfield. As one came into the village from the city end, there was a road to the right called Telok Pekot Road. This road led, via the bottom end of the runway, to Changi beach. The beach was a well known spot for the locals to go during the weekends, not to mention the servicemen. The beach led all the way round to the other side of the village to a place called Changi Point. Changi Point was where the Changi River met the sea. The water flowed from the river into the sea. It was at this point where the two waters met that the waters became very treacherous, with heavy undercurrents. It was also another place where atrocities had occurred during the Japanese occupation. Across the river from the Point was the back of the transit block for families. It was at the front of the transit block, that I had first stopped on arriving at Changi. Just up from the mouth of the river was a small concrete bridge for people to cross from the village onto the beachside of the river. There was also a small jetty where the local fishermen would land their day's catch, to sell in the local fish market. It was also the place where visitors (mostly servicemen) could board boats to go across to Pulau Ubin, *(Pulau* in Malay, means island) or to several other small islands that were dotted along the coast of east Singapore.

When leaving the river to go back towards the village, one would come out at the top end of the village. To get back to the main road one would have to follow an old muddy side street. (All the side streets were muddy during the wet season.) This particular street was quite wide in comparison to the others. In it stood the only cinema, (Changi cinema) in the village. It was the area's flea pit, where all the locals would go to see their own type of films, which would be in their own language, be it Chinese, Hindustani or Pakistani. Most of the side streets in Changi during the monsoon season would be sodden wet, and it was not recommended to walk down them until dry. Once the torrential rain had stopped, the heat in the atmosphere would give off a haze, and one could see the ground steaming dry.

As I said earlier the village itself was a very pleasant place to be in. Everything that anyone would require could be purchased there, from clothes, to hiring cars. Obviously there were bars. One bar that was a favourite place that many Servicemen frequented, was Milly's Bar.

There were also a couple of Chinese barbers. I remember having my haircut at one of them. This occurred about once a fortnight. It was something that I didn't mind having done, as the haircut would take about twenty minutes to half an hour. Not only did you get your haircut, but also, what was called a dry shampoo and massage. The shampoo was put on your hair after you had it cut, was the part that I enjoyed most, because the shampoo used (bay rum) would give your scalp a tingling sensation, and the barber would massage your head for at least a quarter of an hour, or more. Many a time I used to fall asleep whilst having my head massaged. It was absolute ecstasy.

Another place that was frequented by a lot of Servicemen was Fred's Café. Fred was of Indian or Pakistani descent. He owned a small two-wheeled cart, from which he used to serve coffee, tea, and the best jam butties one could ever wish to taste. This cart was situated approximately half way down on the right of the village, across a small muddy alleyway. I call it an alleyway, but in truth it was really a pathway about four feet wide, or even narrower. How he used to stay open virtually all the time service personnel were around I do not know. He would be open most afternoons and all through the night. He use to serve his coffee in a glass beaker, and his jam butties were so big that one was a meal on its own. Many a serviceman would end up at Fred's Café after a booze up, sometimes just to sober up before going back to his billet to kip down.

There were two or three camera shops also in the village. One of the camera shops that were frequented was George's Cameras. He had outside his shop a placard, advertising 'no shit prices'. In other words, his shop was the cheapest in the village for any commodity in the photography line. Once again films and the like were sometimes bought on the knock.

The atmosphere in the village was something else. There was a magical, yet mystical air there. Often when passing a Chinese household one could smell a joss-stick burning, especially during the night. But, of course, it could be smelt during the day as well. There was also the smell of the locals cooking their own favourite dishes – fish – spices, or the odour of coffee. Mixed with these smells was the smell of oil lamps burning, especially during the evenings. Every now and then one would hear the sound of laughter coming from one part of the village or other.

Once the shops had shut, which undoubtedly was always late in the evenings, it was nothing to walk along the pathways in front of the shops only to pass some of the shopkeepers lying on their make shift beds in front of their shops, fast asleep. It was far better to sleep in the open air than indoors during the more humid nights. Considering there was always a little bit more air moving outside, I could understand them doing this and it was always more humid after a downpour of rain, or during the monsoon season.

What with the hot humid days and nights, all the time one could hear the tropical noises around you, from the loud crickets, to birds of all types. At night the bird noises would quieten, and their in its place would be the bull-frogs croaking away along with the crickets and insects flying around.

Chapter Twelve

Aircraft Guard

PERIODICALLY A 'V' bomber would arrive, *en route* to the Woomera Rocket Range in Australia, or other destination.

As is usual during your term at any RAF camp, one was expected to spend at least one day or night on camp, on aircraft guard. It was my misfortune to have to do my little stint roughly three months after arriving in Changi. Along with me, were half a dozen other unfortunate erks due to be on duty. Our job was to guard three Valiant bombers, and a Bristol Britannia cargo plane. We were instructed to make sure that the temperature in the Britannia was not to go over or below sixty Fahrenheit. If for any reason the temperature was go either way, we would have to inform the Duty Corporal, and he in turn would have to inform the Duty Officer immediately.

The Britannia had a few passenger seats inside, so it was decided that, as the temperature inside the aircraft was nice and cool, those of us that were not doing their two-hour stint of two hours on and four hours off would kip down in the Britannia. This meant that there would always be two erks outside guarding the four aircraft. It was obvious that we would team up with someone we knew.

The four of us settled down in the aircraft. Some went to have a look up front at the cockpit, to see what differences there were to the other type of aircraft that came in. Some just got their heads down, played cards; or read a book or magazine; this seemed to be the usual occupation when we were all tied up on guard duty, or when time had to be wasted.

After doing my first two-hour guard I entered the Brit to have a rest. As it was rather humid outside I felt rather thirsty. Knowing that there was a refrigerated drinking tap in the galley of the aircraft for people to have a cool drink, I found a plastic cup at the side of the drinking tap, and poured a cup full of water. To my surprise, the water tasted very similar to the water at home. It then came to me, that the aircraft must have taken this water on board at Lyneham. Which meant that the water had come from the Bristol waterworks plant near RAF Lyneham.

'Talk about being home!' I exclaimed to the others.

'What are you on about?' said Ted, one of the resting erks asked.

'This water is Bristol water. It's got the same texture as out of our taps at home,' I went on.

'You're talking out of your head,' said another.

'No I'm not. It's nice n' cold and really refreshing,' I said. 'I can also tell by the taste.'

Then Ted came up and took a swig of water from my cup. 'Here, he's right!' said Ted. 'It's certainly not from around these 'ere parts. For a start, it's not so soft as yer in-camp. I think he might be bleedin' well right. It's like the water I got at Locking, whilst I was there training.'

With that I was shoved out of the way, and had three or four of the aircraft inhabitants pushing to get a cup of water, as if it was the only thing that had come from Blighty.

As each took a swig of water there came comments like, 'Bloody hell. This is nectar.' Or, 'This is beautiful, sooner have this than Tiger.'

'Hey! Mike, where did you say you think this water is from?' said one of the other erks.

'If I'm not mistaken, I reckon that the water is from my part of the country. Bristol.' I said with pride. 'To think that I would be drinking Bristol water, ten thousand kilometres away. All I need is a bottle of cider. Then I shall think I'm home in Blighty.'

For a while Bristol water was the subject of discussion, until in the end the subject had been exhausted. Everyone on board the aircraft settled down for the night, except for the two erks outside on guard. I had about two and a half hours to go before it was my turn again to go outside on guard in the hot humid night.

During the night around two am, everything was quiet and still. The camp was now asleep, except for those who had the misfortune of being on duty in their separate sections. I for one was just dozing off on board the Brit, after coming off guard only half an hour before.

In my state of semi-conciousness I heard a voice outside shout a warning. 'Halt! Who's there?' Then a moment later, 'Halt! Who's there?' came the voice again followed by 'Come on. Stop fucking about. HALT! Who goes there? If you don't stop, I'll fire!'

The sound of the bolt of the Lee Enfield was then heard to be pulled back. Bang! came the sound of the rifle as it was fired.

The sound of the rifle going off brought everyone to their senses. All in the aircraft made a dash for the door of the plane.

'Stay where you are,' came the command from the Duty Corporal in charge of the guard. 'Everyone sit down and stay down until told to do otherwise.'

The Corporal poked his head out of the aircraft. 'Edwards!' he shouted. 'What the bloody hell is going on?' he enquired.

'I don't know, Corp,' said Edwards outside. 'Saw some movement over there by the second Valiant.'

'What was it then?'

'I don't really know,' Edwards continued. 'I couldn't see it properly. It was a moving shadow under the second bomber. The trouble is that the floodlights ain't on the planes properly, because the tree branches are obscuring the lighting,' Edwards finished.

'Where's Fisher, your partner?' asked the Corporal.

'He's over on the other side of air movements,' Edwards confessed, as he pointed to the other side of the parking bay.

As he was saying this Fisher came running back to find out what was going on.

'Where you been, Fisher?' shouted the Corporal.

'Who's fired his rifle?' enquired Fisher, still out of breath from his run. Then, looking towards his partner, he said, 'Not you Brian? What was it – an accident?'

'No,' said Brian Edwards. 'I saw some movement under the second bomber. So I challenged the movement twice. Had no reply, so I took a pot shot at the shadow.'

'Bloody hell. You're a right prick, I don't think you know what you've done.'

'I was only doing what my instructions are Corporal,' said Edwards. 'I challenged twice, and on the third time, as I didn't get a reply. I fired.'

By now the Corporal was getting really annoyed. 'You cunt! before you fired didn't you think to give me a shout? Don't you realise that

all this means a load of paperwork AND a bloody great enquiry! JUST
FOR ONE POXY BULLET.'

'Now fan out, all of you, and find out what was under that bleeding
plane,' the Corporal gave the order. 'Graves, go and phone up the
Duty Officer, and tell him that we've had an incident here.'

The rest of the guard that were on the plane started to go towards
the bomber in one mass.

'Fan out you bloody fools. We don't know whether it's a Communist
infiltrator, or what yet,' shouted the Corporal as he watched us all
walking towards the plane.

At these instructions, I think most of us came to our senses and
realised the seriousness of the situation. Needless to say, we all jumped
a bit more quickly and fanned out. Some out towards the middle of
the parking bay; some carried on towards the planes, some of us,
(including myself) scrambled up a bank that surrounded the parked
planes, and towards the trees at the top of the bank. All of us using as
much cover as was possible. One individual got himself into the
monsoon drain, and crawled nervously along the foot-deep drain
towards the aircraft. Eventually, a couple of the guards arrived at the
point where Edwards had said he had seen movement. A cry came up.
'I don't know what it was you saw Brian, but your round must have
injured it, because there's some blood here.'

'I told you Corporal. I told you I saw some movement over here,'
cried Edwards in jubilation, as if he had scored a prize.

'Bloody hell,' came the cry from the erk who had crawled along the
monsoon drain. 'Who's pissed into this drain? I'm fucking wet as
buggery.' The erk stood up in the monsoon drain, as he started to
brush himself down.

'That ain't no piss!' said another erk. 'That's blood.'

Everyone started to laugh at the unfortunate erk who now stood
wet in the monsoon drain. 'Perhaps the bloke that just pissed in the
drain has Goners, and is pissing blood,' came a remark from the back.
Everyone started to laugh again.

'Alright, alright, you men. Fan out, and less of the hilarity,' came
the order from a voice in the background. It was the Duty Officer,
who had arrived. 'Everyone make a semi-circle around the aircraft at
regular intervals. No one – and I mean no-one – is to come past you.
Even if it's God Almighty himself who tries to pass you without my
say-so.'

As everyone was getting themselves into position as ordered, a cry came out from the top of the bank near some trees. 'I got the intruder. I got him. He's dead. You shot him Edwards, alright.' The voice that was coming from the top of the bank sounded mocking. 'It's coming down,' came the voice.

With a thud on the concrete below, the body of a monkey fell into view of the floodlights of the parking bay. Everyone started to laugh out loud again. Partly because of the humorous side of it all, and also partly because it released some of the tension that had built up over the last few minutes or so.

'Quiet there,' ordered the Officer. 'Edwards, Fisher, and you Corporal. Come with me,'. The Officer started to walk towards the air movements offices. The three named airmen followed as instructed.

'Webber!' shouted the Corporal. 'You're in charge until I come back.' As he turned to walk towards the offices, he added, 'And don't forget to keep a tight rein on the temperature in that Britannia.'

Everyone else settled down again back on the aircraft. There was an air of hilarity amongst us all. The situation was discussed over and over again on board the aircraft in a very lighthearted manner. Soon it was my turn to go back on duty outside the Britannia for another two hours at least.

Next morning, we were released from guard duty and we all went our separate ways to our individual blocks for a nice comfortable sleep.

I was woken up at around midday by Ted, who had been on guard with me the night before.

'Mike, Brian Edwards has been put on a charge,' he said as he was shaking me out of my sleep.

'What are you on about?' I replied. 'How can he be put on a charge for doing his job last night?'

'That's not what he's been put on a charge for,' explained Ted. 'He's been put on a charge for damaging Her Majesty's property,' he concluded.

'What are you on about?' I repeated as I semi-sat up, resting my elbow on the pillow.

'You know that round that Brian let off and hit the monkey.' Ted started again.

'So?' I nodded.

'Well that round must have gone through the monkey, ricocheted off the concrete and went up through the tail plane of the Valiant behind,' Ted went on.

'I can't see how he can be responsible for that. He was only doing his job. And besides,' I continued. 'If that monkey really had been a communist sympathiser, he would have been awarded a medal.'

'I can't see how they can make this charge stick,' I went on. 'No! I reckon it's a paper exercise. If you remember the Corporal cussed him blind, and said he didn't realise what he was about to start, and that there would be an enquiry, plus a load of paperwork. I'm sure that's all it's about,' I was convinced of my own opinion. 'You wait and see,' I finished off.

'Perhaps you may be right,' said Ted. 'I hope you are. But that's not the impression I got from the others who told me.'

'Who told you?' I asked.

'The chap who sleeps next to him in his billet,' Ted started again. 'From what I can make out, this chap came over to my billet to tell me that Brian Edwards had been escorted to his billet by the RAF police to pick up his things, and was escorted back to the guardhouse. Also, that he had told him that he was being put on a charge for and I quote:- "Damaging Her Majesty's property," unquote.'

'Anyway,' I started again. 'How did they find the bullet hole in the aircraft? Because nothing had been found when we left this morning.'

'From all accounts,' Ted told me, 'after we left this morning the whole area was completely cordoned off and put out of bounds for all personnel, and it was guarded by the RAF Regiment. It was during a complete search of the area they noticed that hole in the tail of the "V" bomber.' He went on, 'I can only suppose that they're looking for the bullet that Brian fired.'

'That's like looking for needle in a haystack. It could have gone anywhere on the airfield, not just around the aircraft concerned. Have they found the bullet? I bet they haven't,' I asserted.

'No, it's all a paper exercise, just to say a full enquiry has taken place,' I concluded.

'Perhaps you're right,' Ted said as he started to leave me to go to his own room. 'I hope you are,' I heard as he went out the door. With that, he was gone.

A few days later, it came out that I had been totally wrong with my verdict. Brian Edwards was charged with Damaging Her Majesty's Property, and was put inside for a little while.

I always felt, during my period in the RAF and after, that this was one of the few occasions when I felt that justice in the services had not been done.

Chapter Thirteen

Unusual and Funny Experiences

MANY TIMES BEFORE I came into the services, I'd heard from other ex-servicemen that one would always remember the good times, and forget the bad times. How right those ex-servicemen were. Most of my memories were very happy ones, which included some really funny moments.

I was fortunate in that, although there were some troubles out in the Far East – like the tail-end of the troubles with President Sukaino of Indonesia – and there was also some trouble brewing up in Cambodia, Laos and Vietnam. I, in my trade, would probably not be required for posting to any places one could call hostile. So my experiences were mostly in Singapore. In the early part of my stay in Singapore I found that I was forever perspiring, mainly under the armpits, and around the groin. As time went by, although showering often and trying to dry myself, I began to get an irritation between the legs, which seemed to be getting worse. I used to use talcum powder to try to eradicate my perspiration after showering. But all to no avail; my groin began to get red, and very sore. I was beginning to wonder if I had crabs or something. Some of my mates in the billet said that I more than likely had 'Tinea'. I would have to see the MO eventually.

I didn't particularly want to do this, because I knew that the treatment for this illness was to have a khaki-green paste put all over the affected area. It was messy, and on top of this, it looked most repulsive. I continued to try and treat myself for a few more weeks, but the redness had now started to turn black. It had become so embarrassing that I couldn't even put a pair of swimming trunks on, because it was also beginning to spread down the inside of my legs.

My situation was becoming beyond a joke. The soreness was now excruciating and the only way I could try to relieve the uncomfortable situation was to sit in the shower with my legs open and let the cold water run onto them. In the end, I had no alternative but to go and see the MO.

On arrival at his office the usual formalities were dealt with, like name, rank, trade, etc. I was then ushered into to see the Medical Officer.

'What's wrong with you, Airman?' he asked.

'I think I have Tinea, sir!' I replied.

'Oh, and where have you Tinea?' the Officer asked.

'Between the legs, sir,' I answered.

'Right! Drop them.' the Officer ordered.

I dropped my shorts, as I had been instructed. The Officer looked between my legs and felt the infected area. As he touched me, I winced with pain, giving a quiet curse.

'How long have you been like this my son?' the MO enquired. 'I'd say you've been like this for quite some while.'

'About a month I would think, sir,' I answered.

'You've been like this for a bit longer than a month,' he said as a statement of fact. 'Why haven't you been to see me before?'

'Because, sir, I didn't want to bother you,' I paused, and then as an afterthought continued. 'on top of that, sir, I thought I might try to cure myself.'

'Anything else, Airman?' the MO looked at me with a frown.

I started off slowly. 'Well, sir . . .'

'Y-e-e-es?' said the MO equally slowly.

'Well, sir. I didn't particularly want to put on any of that khaki-coloured paste, that you have, sir,' I finished.

'Now we're coming to the truth', the MO affirmed. 'Well, for your information, you have caused yourself a lot of unnecessary pain and discomfort. Because we haven't used that khaki-coloured paste for a while,' he stated, as he proceeded towards the cabinet. He drew out a small bottle of clear liquid. 'Put this on twice a day with some cotton wool, or with a clean handkerchief,' he instructed. 'I warn you, however, this ointment will sting a little.'

'Thank you, sir,' I replied. Saluting the MO I came out of the building. I was feeling rather pleased with myself, because I had got away with not having to use that horrible paste.

Once I got back to the billet, I took out a clean handkerchief from my cabinet beside the bed, opened the bottle of liquid that the MO had handed to me, and tipped some of the contents onto it. I then proceeded to dab the handkerchief between my legs, onto the affected area.

'BLOODY HELL!' I cried out loud.

Sting was not the word for it. I literally jumped into the air about ten feet, when the liquid seemed to burn into my leg. I had only touched one part of the black sore mass between my legs, and that was only on the edge. I had to soak all of the affected area. Each time I touched the sore, I jumped into the air with anguish. God, it was painful. The good thing about it, luckily for me, was that by the next morning, the soreness had subsided, and that was with only one or two administrations. I bathed my groin all over again next day, jumping on each occasion I dabbed the sore. By the time a week had passed I found that the sore had more or less disappeared. Was I pleased about that! It had been the worst experience of a tropical infection that I'd had, and I didn't ever intend to have it again. It also taught me a lesson, and that was not to wait in future before seeing the MO.

During my days off I had reason to join the camp's local broadcasting system. Commonly known as the CBS (Changi Broadcasting System). I had the chance of broadcasting for a half hour, weekly programme called *Anything Goes,* in which I could select my own records. Here my broad Bristol/Somerset accent I was finding to be an asset.

One afternoon, I was seated outside the back of the broadcasting building selecting the records for my next broadcast, when a WRAF came up to me.

'You Mike Baker?' she enquired.

'Yep! that's me,' I replied.

'You come from Bristol, don't you?' she said as a statement of fact.

I returned with, 'Well, yes I do. But anyone can tell you this just by listening to my accent.'

She retorted. 'Yes, but you used to work for the GPO didn't you?'

'Yes I did, as a messenger boy,' I answered. 'But how did you know this?'

'I'll tell you something else as well,' she continued. 'Can you remember going up to Birmingham with the messengers for a football competition against the Birmingham messengers?'

My ears pricked up at the last statement. 'How do you know that?' I asked.

'I haven't finished yet,' she started again. 'You went up there with three other of your mates.' She named the three mates whom I had been with on that particular day out.

'How in the devil do you know all this,' I asked. By now I was completely mystified, and wondered how she knew all about me, not thinking of the obvious.

'On the way back,' she went on, 'you all sat in the back row of seats, with four girls.'

All this was completely true.

'Yes, that's quite correct. We met up with these girls on the way up to Birmingham,' I commented. 'But how do know all this about me?' I was by now entirely dumbfounded.

'Come on.' I started again. 'Don't keep me in suspense. How in the hell do you know all this about me?'

'You really don't recognise me do you, Mike Baker'? she said laughing.

'No, I'm sorry, but I don't.

'Well I was one of the girls that was in the back seat with you,' she explained.

'That must have been all of five years ago.'

'Yes! I suppose it must be,' she agreed. 'Anyway, I've a photograph at home that was taken with all of us together. I'll get my mum to send it out to me, just to prove that I'm not lying.'

'That should be interesting to see.'

We went on talking for quite a while after about one thing or another, until it was time to go our separate ways.

A couple of weeks later, sure enough, she came into the broadcasting system, and produced the photograph that her mother had sent out.

'There you are, Mike Baker. I wasn't kidding you on. There's you on the left with your arm around one of the girls,' she pointed out. 'And there's me with John in the centre,' she finished. All I could do was agree with her, because without doubt, there I was on the day in question. What a small world it is becoming. Ten thousand kilometres away, and I'm still meeting people from years ago. What with Maureen Sheppard on the aircraft journey out here, and now this WRAF . . .

Very often, when we had nothing very much to do, due to us having to go on duty within an hour or so, or, for some other reason, some of the lads, on the top floor of block 144 would sometimes go into the middle lounge. Now and then, they would put the radio on, or put a record on the radiogram that had been installed there. On other occasions they would go in there, just to look at a newspaper, or a magazine. Anything to relax, or while the time away.

One afternoon, after coming off duty, I happened to be changing from my uniform, into some more casual attire, before going on my way to the swimming pool down at the Pogar, when I heard some music coming from the middle lounge. The music sounded very familiar, but couldn't put my finger on where I had heard it before. I started to hum the part that I recognised. Suddenly, it came to me. It was the theme music from the sci-fi series on television a few years earlier. It was *The Quatermass Experiment*. I walked into the lounge, where sat in one of the easy chairs was Paul Coxswain. He was listening to a record. Paul was a rather stocky, but short fellow. He was a bit of a professor. He had been born in India, through his father being posted there in the army and he could speak several languages. Amongst them were Hindustani, Malay, German and a couple of the Chinese dialects.

'Where did you buy that piece of music Paul? That's from *The Quatermass Experiment*' I asked him. I had interrupted his listening, and he replied in a rather chastising tone.

'Some of you blokes are a load of crap. You don't appreciate good music when you bleeding well hear it.'

'I'm sorry,' I said. Holding my hands and arms out beside me. 'What are you on about. What have I said?'

'You lot make me mad. All you lot think is that music is written for television,' he said, as he stood up, glowering at me.

'I'm sorry,' repeating myself. 'All I asked was where you got that piece of music from, because it was from *The Quatermass Experiment*. That's all. Furthermore,' I added. 'I happen to like that particular piece of music.'

Paul seemed to calm down at my additional comment about liking that particular music.

'Mike! Don't you know anything about classical music?' he asked.

'No, not a lot. It's a little bit too highbrow for me,' I replied.

'Let me tell you something for your education, shall I,' Paul started.

'That piece of music that you say is from *The Quatermass Experiment*. Has been taken from a well known classic, namely *The Planets Suite* by Gustav Holst. Also, for your education, that particular piece of music is called *Mars, Bringer of War*.'

'Well, I still like it, regardless,' I said. 'What did you say it was called?' I asked again, because I hadn't taken it all in, on the first occasion. Paul repeated the information. He then went on to tell me that most of the theme music on television series was in actual fact taken from classical music and adapted. He then went on to give examples of theme music for different TV series, and where they originated.

I came out of that lounge that afternoon, very much more educated as to classical music. In fact, it was my first initiation into classical music, and I have never stopped loving it since.

Part of service life at Christmas time was a tradition, carried out for many years, even during the First World War, that the Officers would wait on the Servicemen, the main tradition being for the Officers to serve the Christmas lunch to their men.

Our Flight Sergeant from Com-cen Changi invited around six to ten single Servicemen, who were billeted at the camp to his home in Siglap (a suburb of Singapore City) for Christmas lunch. His home was a flat on the fourth floor. We had to be there on Christmas Day between 11.30 and 12.00 hours. We all duly arrived at the appointed time. Each was offered a drink of his choice. Some had Anchor beer, others Coca-Cola and what have you. I, on my part had, as many others did, Tiger beer. Quite a considerable amount of liquid refreshment had been consumed by the time we all sat down for our Christmas meal and everyone was in very inebriated mood.

The Flight Sergeant's wife did us proud, with all the usual Christmas refinements – like Christmas crackers, funny hats and the like. After the meal, some of us, including myself, went back to our favourite pastime, drinking and were, to put it mildly, a little the worse for wear.

Colin Summers, one of the Com-cen crew, asked me, 'What's the time Mike?'

I looked at my watch through glassy eyes. 'Oh, about 3.30. Why?'

'Hell's bells!' he cried. 'I'm supposed to be on duty at 13.00 hours.'

As he was crying this statement out, he was rushing towards the front door. 'Bleeding hell, I'll get Court Martialled for this.' As he went out the door everyone else laughed at his misdemeanour.

I went to the front window which looked out onto the main road. This had four lanes of traffic, with a broad white line down through the middle of it which allowed two lanes of traffic to flow in each direction. The traffic was very heavy, as if it was rush hour in some of our busy cities at home.

I watched Colin Summers running up the middle of the road on the broad white line, with a glass of ordinary beer in one hand and a bottle of Tiger beer in the other, the traffic passing him in both directions very close, with cars sounding their horns at him. He, in his drunken state, tried to hail a taxi from the middle of the road, whilst running in the direction of Changi camp. The last I saw of Colin that day was watching him running up the middle of the road, on the white line calling 'Taxi! Taxi!' with his arms flailing about. Everyone in the flat could see the funny side of his predicament, including the Flight Sergeant and his wife.

Next morning, I remember waking up, looking around me, only to find each side of me was a wall of green. Where the heck am I? I thought. I must be dreaming. The light was bright, and I tried to shield my eyes with my hands. My head was heavy and throbbing and I felt like nothing on earth. Where the bleeding hell am I? I thought again. Whilst I was thinking this I was trying to scramble up out of bed, only to find that I was not in bed, but in a very deep gully. Each time I tried to get up, I fell back down. I was on my knees, and tried once more to get myself out of the predicament I was in. I didn't know what time it was and I didn't know where I was. I could have been anywhere in Singapore.

'Good morning Airman,' came a voice from nowhere.

'Who the f*** is that?' I enquired.

'Have you had a good night's sleep, Airman?' the voice enquired, in a rather sarcastic manner.

'Who the f*** is that?' I raged again, adding, 'Where the bloody hell am I?'

'Don't you know where you are, Airman?' went on the voice, in answer to my questions, and still in a mocking tone.

'No! I bloody well don't know where I am,' I cried out.

'You must have had a brilliant Christmas Day. Airman, you were pissed as a coot when you arrived here yesterday evening,' the voice went on.

'Oh hells bells. Where the f***, am I?' I started again. 'Stop pissing about and tell me where the hell I am.'

The voice was laughing at me. 'You honestly don't know where you are?' The voice asked.

'No! I bloody well don't know where I am,' I started again, as I held my head at the same time trying to see who I was talking to. 'The last place I remember was the Flight Sergeant's house at Siglap,' I finished, 'and that was about 4.00 o'clock this afternoon.'

'That was yesterday. It is now 10.00 hours on Boxing Day, Sunshine,' came the voice. 'Come here. Let me help you out of the monsoon drain.'

'Derrick! He's awake. Come and give me a hand to get him out.'

Next moment, an RAF police Officer jumped down to help me out of the monsoon drain. 'You must have had a skinful yesterday my ol' mate,' the RAF copper said, as he got hold of me and started to push my backside up the slope of the drain. Another hand from above reached out to grab hold of me to help pull me up. 'Come on, mate. I've seen it all now. Come on into the guardroom, and have a coffee,' said the RAF policeman.

After I had been pulled out of the ditch, I looked around me, through rather glazed eyes, and a thick head, and found that I had been in the six-foot deep monsoon ditch; the green being the grass on each side of the drain. I was also just inside the gates of RAF Changi, and right outside the guardroom.

I was helped up the steps to the guardroom by both the RAF coppers. As I entered the guardroom, a big cheer came from inside. 'You drunken ol' bum,' all the occupants of the guardroom were laughing at me. Personally, I couldn't have cared less, because my head was in no state to care. It was still throbbing like hell and every sound seemed as if it was coming over a very large Tannoy. My mouth was as dry as could be.

I was handed a cup of coffee which I thanked them for. The RAF copper who had helped me out of the monsoon drain asked, 'How did you get in the state you were in last night?'

I answered that I didn't know anything from about 16.00 hours after watching my mate running up the main road after a taxi at about 15.00 hours. I couldn't remember leaving Siglap. I couldn't remember how I got back to camp. I couldn't remember anything. It was the first time I had got myself into such a paralytic drunken state. One of the occupants of the guardroom retorted, 'Well! you won't forget the first time you ever got pissed, that's for sure.'

He was certainly right.

Every now and then I used to go for a flight in a Shackleton Mk. 2 aircraft – purely for the ride, but officially as an 'observer.' One particular day, the Flieght Lieutenant, (I knew him as Jeff) that I generally went with came into the Com-cen and asked me, 'Mike! Are you coming with us next Friday morning? That's assuming you're not working.'

I replied, 'Sure, if you want me on this trip. Anyway, where are we going? The usual flight?'

'Yes, as usual. The North and South China Seas,' he said with a sigh. 'Anyway, that's not why I came to see you.'

'Oh?' I said looking at him a little puzzled. 'Well, what did you want to see me for?' I enquired.

'Well, you won't be the only passenger, and I want you to look after the other guy before we take off,' Jeff said.

'OK OK. Who is it?' I said laughing.

'For some reason or other, we got a matelot on this trip,' Jeff said in a rather questioning tone.

'What's he want a flight for?' I asked.

'I don't know,' Jeff answered slowly. 'Anyway, he's to report to next door (next door to the Com-cen) at 06.00 hours,' Jeff went on. Then, looking at me in the eyes, 'Can you take him down to the parachute hangar to draw the necessary, please.'

'Sure,' I said. 'That's no problem. I got to go down there to get my own anyway, as you know.'

'Cheers Mike,' Jeff said, smiling, as if it were a weight off his mind. With that he left.

On the Friday, I arrived outside the Flight Planning Office, which was next door to the Com-cen. Sitting quietly in the corner was a sailor. 'Are you coming on a flight with us this morning?' I questioned the matelot.

'Yes! That's right,' he answered.

'Well, I'm Mike Baker,' I greeted him as I put my hand out to shake his.

'And I'm Tony Croner,' he introduced himself, as we shook hands.

'Well Tony, I've been given the job of looking after you until we get on board the Shack,' I said to him.

Tony was about five feet seven inches tall, and looked a little ill at ease. He was dressed in his uniform, but didn't look at all happy. I would say he was of a nervous disposition.

'Ever been in an aircraft before Tony?' I asked him, trying to get him to relax.

'No,' he replied, rather quietly.

'Oh it's great,' I replied excitedly. 'You'll love it.'

'Will I?' He said sheepishly.

'Come on, come with me,' I beckoned him out of the door. 'You'll love it. Honest. There's nothing like flying,' I said, encouraging him as we went out of the door.

'Why do you say that?' he asked.

'Because you will love it. There's nothing like it. You wait and see,' I replied.

'Look Mike,' Tony began. 'Its not that I'm frightened of flying, or anything like that. In fact I'm looking forward to it in a way.'

'Well! Why are you looking so nervous then?' I asked.

'As I said, I've never flown before. I'm excited in one way, but apprehensive in another,' Tony concluded.

'Oh-h-h,' I said in a comforting tone of voice. 'There's nothing to flying. What are you apprehensive about then?' I enquired.

'I don't know really,' Tony said, rather grudgingly. 'What happens if something goes wrong while we're flying? Suppose an engine breaks down, or two even.'

I stopped dead in my tracks, turned to him, and said as I put both hands on his shoulders, 'Look Tony! nothing's going to happen. A Shackleton can fly for twenty-four hours non-stop, and on top of that it has four engines,' I said. 'Also, for your information, it's one of very few planes that, if necessary, can fly on one engine. It's got four engines as I said, and each engine has twin propellers.'

'How do you know it can fly on only one engine?' Tony enquired. 'Have you seen it fly on one engine?' he asked.

'As a matter of interest, yes! I have. 205 Squadron do it very often around this airfield as practice,' I said indignantly. 'So there's nothing to worry about.'

That seemed to reassure Tony.

'Where are we making for?' he asked, as we walked along the road.

'Oh, not far,' I replied, nonchalantly. I had a feeling that the answer to the next question was going to put Tony right off the thoughts of flying again.

'Where then?' Tony asked again.

'We're going to get a parachute,' I then started to laugh, because I could see the funny side after our conversation. 'Just in case something goes wrong and we have to bale out.'

Tony went ashen white.

'It's alright. We all have to have one. It's just regulations, nothing more,' I tried to console him and he seemed to take a little comfort from the reason for the issue of parachutes.

We went into the parachute hangar, and as we entered I had a feeling that the fun was about to start. Everyone in there turned and looked at Tony, wondering what he was doing in the RAF's domain. I went up to the nearest Corporal and said 'Two parachutes to be drawn, please.' The Corporal winked at me, and asked quietly, because Tony was standing a little back from me, 'What's he doing here?'

'Search me,' I said quietly. 'All I know is he's shit-scared of flying,' I went on, 'I don't know why he's here, because he's so knotted up.'

'I take it you want the normal procedure carried out?' said the Corporal.

I knew what he meant by the last comment.

'Yes please,' I said.

The Corporal meant by this, that the matelot was to have the full treatment when it came to fitting the parachute as per regulations.

I signed for my parachute, and duly hung it over my shoulder.

'This is Tony!' I introduced him to the Corporal. 'A matelot going for his first flight with me today.'

'Hi!' said the Corporal. 'It's my job to kit you up with a parachute.'

'Hi,' replied Tony. 'Thank you.'

The Corporal started to show Tony how to fit a parachute on, what to do if he had to use it, where to pull the ripcord and so on. All the time, Tony was looking even more white and scared, worrying in case something went wrong on the flight. The Corporal had Tony kitted out with the parachute on him. All the straps had been put around and under his legs. The parachute pouch, or bag, was lying at the back of Tony's legs.

Different things were being said, and I could feel that a certain question was almost bound to come from Tony. Finally, it did.

'What happens if I have to jump?' said Tony.

'Ye-e-s,' said the NCO, as he looked over towards me, and winked.

'And the parachute don't open for me as I fall towards the ground,' Tony finished.

'Oh-h-h. That's no problem,' said the Corporal. 'No problem at all.'

'No?' said Tony, in a rather vacant manner.

' No-o-o-o' replied the Corporal, shaking his head. 'If your parachute don't open when you have to bale out at five thousand feet or so, just bring it back and we'll replace it for you.'

Before anyone could start laughing. Tony looked up, and said so innocently. 'Oh.'

Everyone including myself started to laugh out loud. Tony couldn't see what everyone was laughing at.

'Come on, Tony,' I said to him though still laughing at him. 'Before you drop yourself in more trouble.'

We walked out of the parachute hangar, both carrying our parachutes. You could hear everyone laughing in the hangar as we left. I was laughing as well, and still Tony couldn't see what the joke was all about.

'What are you all laughing at? Have I said, or done something I shouldn't have?' asked poor old Tony.

'Tony,' I said as I stopped walking, and still laughing. 'Tony, if you don't know what you said, and why everyone was laughing at you in the parachute hangar by now, you never will.'

'Well what did I say in the hangar?' asked Tony.

I was beginning to wonder if Tony had been set up to go on this flight as a gag by his own mates. I decided to spell it out to him as best I could.

'Tony, you never ask a question about what you can do if your parachute doesn't open,' I said. 'Think about it,' I said scathingly to him.

Finally we got to 205 squadron, and we were duly met by Jeff and the rest of the crew whom I had got to know reasonably well from earlier flights. We took off for the North and South China Seas for the normal fifteen-hour flight, patrolling for anything that might look illegal or for ships that could look like pirates. Things of that nature.

Pirates in the China Seas were not all that common, but did occur now and then. Usually the pirates would attack other slow-moving ships or boats, similar to Chinese junks.

On this particular flight nothing much happened, and for me it was a rather boring one. Although I enjoyed it, purely because of the flying aspect of it. As for Tony, he was very quiet from the time he was shown where to sit, and how to use his parachute as a cushion to the time we landed that night back at Changi.

The more I think about Tony, the more I think he was set up by his mates at HMS *Terror*. Because he was never flying material, and never will be. He seemed to be as white as Death when he got off the aircraft. On top of that, he was airsick a few times whilst we were airborne.

One afternoon, at approximately 13.15 hours I and a Royal Malayan Air Force friend were walking up Tangmere Road. We were on our way to the mess for our midday meal, after finishing our stint at the Com-cen. We weren't talking about anything in particular, and not really looking where we were walking, just that we were on the pavement, and to the left of us was a monsoon drain and then the road. The day itself was no different from any other. It was the usual sunny, warm and humid day.

Suddenly, for no reason at all, I appeared to float into the air, and travelled about ten feet further on up the pavement.

Choo came up to me, poised as if to ask me how I had performed this unusual movement. I stopped him and pointed out to where I had just floated over.

There wriggling across the pavement was a small black snake, locally known as a boot lace. It was around twelve inches long and was as thin as a boot lace. Had I been bitten by it my life would not have lasted very long.

Now the incredible thing about the whole incident is this:

1 I did not see the Snake.
2 I did not smell the Snake, and
3 I did not hear the Snake.

How I came to float I just do not know. I certainly didn't jump, or make any attempt to jump whatsoever. What happened that day I have never been able to fathom out, and neither has anyone else that I have spoken to on the subject. It's been a complete mystery.

One of the things that concerned some of the erks who were due to go home to Blighty within a few weeks was how much they had got themselves suntanned. For the majority, there were no problems, as they were darker than the local inhabitants. I for one, was fortunate, and had become as black as the ace of spades, but some weren't so lucky. Due to their skin pigmentation, they would stay white, or almost as white as the day they arrived in Singapore. One of the things that I noticed was that most of them had auburn hair, or freckles. One of these unfortunates was a lad in our billet. His name was Chris Morrison.

Chris was due to go home the following week but as he had seven to ten days' leave still due to him he decided to have his last week's leave in Changi. This was on top of his disembarkation leave. He was a lad with fairish hair, but one could notice there was a hint of ginger there as well. Also, he had freckles all over his body and his skin was almost white, but he was determined to get himself suntanned before going home.

He set up a plan so that he could spend all his leave period day in and day out from sun-up, to sun-down, up on the roof of the billet. He was able to do this due to the billet roof being flat. He was going to take a towel up with him to lie on, and another to wipe the perspiration off himself, if and when he had cause to. It was also arranged with his mates to get his breakfast, lunch, tea, and any drinks that he may so desire throughout the day. That way he would be able to stay up on the roof for the full twelve hours, from seven in the morning, to approximately seven in the evening. sunbathing the whole time.

The first day came. He had arranged to be woken by the fellows who had to go on duty at 08.00 hours. He took his two towels with him, went up onto the roof and stayed there the whole day while his mates fetched, carried his food, and drinks back to him, from the mess.

In the evening, after the sun had gone down, he came down from the roof as pleased as could be. He found that he was red as a cherry.

Next morning he woke up and became a little disappointed, since his redness had gone down. But as there was still some pinkishness there he wasn't too despondent and up he went onto the roof again.

This went on for the whole of his leave period. Every morning he would go up. Each evening, he would come back down. During this time, his mates would look after all his needs. And every evening he was as red as a beetroot. Each morning, he would wake up only to find that he had gone back to his usual pinkish colour.

Finally, the day came for him to go home, back to good old Blighty. After all the time that he had spent on the roof, he went home the same as he came to Changi. Just like a Moonie.

One thing that one could always rely on in the RAF, or any of the services, was the comradeship. Your mates wouldn't let you down under any adiversity whatsoever. If you were in any trouble they would be there to back you up.

One particular day, I remember well was on my birthday, I was completely broke, with not a dollar, or cent to my name.

I was lying on my pit, late in the afternoon, feeling really down in the dumps and thinking. What a way to spend your birthday. Completely broke. No money to celebrate, or nowt. I must have been lying on my bed for at least an hour, getting more morose than ever. I remember being there on my back, with my hands on the back of my head, watching the cool fans rotate. Everything seemed to be quiet apart from the hum of the fan motors. Nobody seemed to be around. The whole place appeared to have been abandoned.

Then in walked John, as if to get something from his locker. 'What are you doing this evening, Mike?' asked John.

'Not a lot,' I answered. 'Why?'

'Well, I thought you might have been celebrating in someway or other. It's your birthday ain't it.'

'You know it's my birthday, but I can't celebrate nowt. Cos I ain't got a nickel to my name,' I said, in a rather moaning tone.

Suddenly, in ran a crowd of guys from different parts of the billet. They pulled me out of my pit. 'Come on,' they cried. 'You're not celebrating your birthday like this.' Before I had chance to do anything they had taken out some clothes from my locker and started to dress me manually.

'I ain't got a cent to spend,' I tried to explain.

'Maybe you haven't got any money to spend, but some of us have. So come on. Let's go and get pissed,' called out John.

They took me down to the Malcolm Club for the rest of the evening I was treated to Tiger and Anchor beer, until it ran out of my ears. That was what comradeship was all about. It was also one of the best birthdays that I have ever spent.

Chapter Fourteen

Singapore City

FROM RAF CHANGI, to Singapore City, as was said earlier, was approximately twenty miles away on the Southern tip of the diamond-shaped island. You could get to Singapore City either by bus, or taxi. If you went by taxi there were two methods. The first method was by the meter system, or the second method, by what was known as a pick up. This way one could barter a price, which would be a lot cheaper than the meter. But the taxi driver would be able to pick-up other passengers *en route*. A bus, or taxi could be boarded anywhere on the Upper Changi Road as this was the main road to Singapore.

On the way to Singapore City one would drive past the well-known and infamous Changi jail. Changi jail was situated on the corner of a cross-roads, but set right back so that there was plenty of ground around it. The road leading to the right led to Lorong and the docks (HMS *Terror*) or in the opposite direction back down to the Changi beach. Straight on, towards Singapore itself.

Changi jail walls were set back approximately a hundred yards from the main road. The walls were very thick: about twenty to thirty feet thick at the base, and about twenty-five foot high, maybe more. Guards were posted every few yards along the top, standing in their small lookout towers. The thickness of the walls were shaped, as you looked at them side on, like a big mushroom, with a large hangover on the top of the walls, so it was very hard for anyone to try to scale. The main gate was built like a fortress gate, thick and massive. It always made me think of the music from Mussorgsky's *Great Gate of Kiev*. The doors were so thick and large, I imagined that it would have taken several men to open them. Inside the walls was a large oblong building, built of massive granite-like stones and several floors high. It looked forbidding and dark. The nearest thing that I can compare it to, would be the main building at Dartmoor prison. Everything about Changi prison had a feeling of doom. One could sense the atmosphere around the building as historic and grotesque, and yet, for all that it had that air of magnanimity.

Most military personnel, regardless of what service they were in, would normally make their first port of call, in the centre of the City, at a place called the Britannia Club. The club was run by the NAAFI and it was also the only place at that time where there was a freshwater swimming pool. The Brit Club as it was generally known, was situated on the corner of Beach Road and Bras Basah Road. It was a real central point for visiting many places. On the opposite corner was the world renowned Raffles Hotel. From the Brit Club one could go to cinemas like the Capital or the Odeon, also, to such places as Bugis Street, the 'Old', 'Happy' and 'New' Worlds, or the colourful Tiger Balm Gardens. There were many, many places of interest and most could be easily reached by walking, taxi, or trishaw.

I remember going to the Brit Club for the first time a few days after arriving from Blighty. I went with a few of my fellow Com-cen friends on the first day I was off duty. We sat down, and were approached by a bar girl who took our orders for drinks. It was the custom in Singapore for all bar girls to take your order, and after bringing the order back, to sit with you as a hostess. It was also a way of getting a few more drinks bought, as invariably the bar girl would be asked if she wished for a drink as well.

After a while, and a few drinks later, my bowels decided that they wished to relieve themselves. I had become a little constipated over the first few days in Singapore. I enquired as to where the Gents was. After being directed, I followed the instructions that I had been given and went downstairs. As I entered the Gents I looked for a vacant closet, found one, and shut the door behind myself. The unfortunate thing was that there were no toilet seats. All there was, was a large concrete block, with a shaped basin in the middle. The concrete had then been covered with small mosaic tiles of approximately half to three-quarter inch diameter, and looked extremely cold. My bowels were by now beginning to grumble more urgently. I dropped my shorts, and very gingerly began to lower myself very slowly onto to the cold-looking mosaic seat, expecting my backside to get a shock on impact. Imagine my surprise and pleasure when my backside came into contact with the mosaic seat. I found it to be quite warm, and not at all as I expected. I had forgotten that I was no longer in a cold climate, but a very warm environment.

Next to the Brit Club were some army barracks. A little further on was the Alhambra Cinema and approximately half way between the two places was a small side street where during the evenings and throughout the day (but more during the evenings and night) a large group of local tradesmen, mostly Chinese, would sell food from small carts. Each cart had a row of wooden seats (basically a plank of wood) along the length of the cart. The tradesman would stand between you and the cart, with a charcoal fire in the middle of the cart.

It was here that I spent many a pleasant evening, and sometimes early mornings. For this was where one could buy the best satay in Singapore.

Satay, for those who do not known is a small piece of meat on a thin skewer of bamboo. You could buy several types of satay: mutton, chicken, or beef. It all cost one cent a stick. The owner of the cart would be barbecuing the satay over the charcoal fire, whilst every now and then fanning the fire with a large oval-shaped bamboo fan. There was always satay available left in front of the fire already cooked. You would be able to help yourself to whatever number of sticks of satay you wished. There were always different dishes of chilli sauces, some hotter than others, to dip your satay into. There were also drinks to buy, from beers to coffee or tea and everything was at a very low price.

Of all the places in Singapore this street had one of the best atmospheres one could imagine. It was lit by the low light of the vendors' oil lamps, and charcoal fires. The street was full with the smell of satay and charcoal smoke. Everyone, from all walks of life came there. (I'll call it Satay Street, because I never really found out what the true name of the street was). One could sat beside a pauper, or beside a millionaire. Everyone was equal. It was nothing to see people come across the road from the Raffles Hotel, and sit beside you in evening dress. The men in white tuxedos, and the women in long flowing gowns, adorned with jewellery. There was no class distinction whatsoever.

Another place that I visited many times during my stay was the infamous Bugis Street (pronounced Boo-gee). Bugis Street was renown for its drinking parlours, its girls and its notoriety. It was also a well-known fact that many a fight would start there amongst military personnel over girls who frequented the area. Invariably, when the fights were started it would more than likely be by matelots (sailors) who had just docked. The men wouldn't know at that time, that the girls that they were fighting over, were in actual fact, men. The problem with the girls was it was, very hard to distinguish whether they were girls or not. They had such beautiful make-up, hair, and dresses, and their physique was so normal, with little breasts, it really was hard to know the difference. They would look absolutely fabulous and it was very easy to be deceived, since they looked so feminine. Even I could not be sure at times. For this reason, I stayed clear of the women of Bugis Street, even though I was tempted very often. I liked going there, partly for the fun, because here too the atmosphere was magical. It was commonly known, that you never, ever went to Bugis Street alone. You always went with a friend. You would find a table at the side of the street, order a drink, and then sit, and watch the world go by. Prostitutes (or the 'girls') would come to your table to sell themselves. Local Chinese merchants would come to sell all manner of merchandise, from cotton to all kinds of materials. Mostly the materials would be Japanese brocade. Young boys, about nine to thirteen years of age, would approach you, with indecent suggestions about their sister. Or, if they didn't say anything about their sister, they would be trying to sell pornographic photographs.

I remember being in Bugis Street one evening, after visiting the cinema. I was with a friend at the time, having a drink at the bottom part of Bugis Street, when all of sudden a commotion started at the top end. This carried on for about a quarter of an hour. Suddenly the street was full of military police (Red Caps). There were several three-ton trucks at the top of the street, and at the bottom. Without any discrimination everyone of Caucasian descent was herded into the back of the trucks. There was no argument, nothing. If you argued, several Red Caps would descend on you, and man-handle you very roughly onto the truck. When the truck was full it was covered over with the flap at the back, so no one knew where they were going, and the back was guarded by two or three burly Red Caps. The truck then set off.

About thirty minutes later the truck came to a halt. We were shouted at, and harangued out of the trucks. I began to think I was back square-bashing again at Bridgnorth. We were ordered to line up outside the guardroom (we were at the general headquarters of the Army) and had to produce our identity cards, regardless of whether we were in uniform or not. Each one of us produced our ID (1250). From our ID cards, we were segregated into the three armed services, the Royal Marines going in with the Navy. Any of the personnel who was found to be a civilian was told go home.

The rest of us, were put into separate rooms. Royal Air Force, in one room. Royal Navy in another, and so on. Approximately an hour later, the door opened and in walked two RAF policemen.

'Which of you lot are at Changi?' Came the question.

'I am!' I replied.

'Right, into back of the Land-Rover,' he ordered me. 'Anyone else?' he asked as I proceeded towards the door.

'I am, as well,' said my mate.

'Anyone else?' I heard him say, as I went out of the door towards the Land-Rover that was parked just outside the door.

In all, there were only four personnel from RAF Changi who had been picked up in Bugis Street that evening. We had all got into the back of the Land-Rover. Eventually the two RAF policemen came out from the guardroom. One of them had a clipboard in his hand.

They both jumped into the front of the Land-Rover, and started the engine, and drove out of the Army camp.

After we left the camp one of the policemen asked, 'What was all that about then?'

One of the erks that was with us, answered, 'We don't really know. All I know is that some fight or other started just down from us. The next thing we knew was that the street was closed, and everyone was put in the back of a three-ton truck and brought to GHQ.'

'While I was in the queue earlier, and I was showing my 1250,' one of the Navy wallahs that was in front of me, said that a fight had started between a matelot and a Marine.'

'How true this is, I don't know,' his mate interjected.

'Bloody stupid,' said the other policeman that was driving the Land-Rover. 'Just over a bloody fight they sent us out, to come and bail you lot out.'

I asked, 'You don't mean to tell me that you have had to come all the way from Changi just for us, have you?'

'Yes we bloody well have. Trust the f**** Navy and Marines to put us on the line! You just can't trust the bastards can you,' came the reply from the driver.

The other policeman, who during this time had been writing on a piece of paper that was attached to his clipboard, asked.

'Anyway, because it wasn't your fault, where do you lot want dropping off?'

'Back to Bugis Street if you don't mind,' I replied.

As the road went right past Bugis Street to go back to Changi, it was no problem for them to drop me and my mate off there.

We got out of the Land-Rover, thanked them for the lift, and proceeded to walk back up to the table we had been so unceremoniously removed from. The Chinese barman came up to us, and asked for our order. My mate looked up, and said, in a rather annoyed tone, 'What happened to the beers we were drinking, before the Red-Caps closed the street?'

'I'm very sorry sir. I didn't recognise you. You come back. I go and get you another drink, on the house,' he said in his very apologetic, broken English.

'You crafty old bleeder you,' I said to my mate. 'We'd more or less finished our drinks when we were picked up.'

'I know that, but he don't,' he said as he pointed to the barman.

Whilst drinking and generally watching the world go by, and having a laugh at this and that, we noticed that in the short time we had returned, most of the personnel that were at GHQ with us, and were in the RAF had come back too, but very few of the other Servicemen. We stayed in Bugis Street for about another hour, before we decided to get a pick-up taxi back to camp.

Another evening I went to Bugis Street. with a friend, Steve Richardson, whom I had met at Changi. He was in the Royal Marines, and belonged to 42nd Commando Group. Forty-second Commando Group had a detachment based at Changi. Every so many weeks, he would go into the jungle on the mainland of Malaya on patrol. The idea of these patrols was to go in search of Indonesian infiltrators, or any enemies of the State. Anyway, Steve and I were sitting in Bugis Street generally watching the world go by, when some of his own mates from the Royal Marines passed by. They stopped, and sat down with us. Ordered a few beers. He introduced me to them, and we all sat together having a laugh and a joke.

There was one individual I'll call John, as I have forgotten his name, who gave the impression of being a right know-all. He wasn't all that old, about eighteen at a rough guess, but was short in stature, around five foot eight tall. Obviously, he knew that I was from the Royal Air Force, and started to bug me about the Royal Marines being the better service, and all that jazz. This inter-service rivalry didn't usually bother me because it was normally all good fun, with no animosity behind it, but on this occasion, it did, partly because he kept on and on and on. I then decided to put one over on him, and make him look a right bleeding idiot, especially among his own mates.

'Here John,' I started. 'You're a Royal Marine aren't you?' I asked.

'Yeah,' said John. 'Everybody know the Marines are the best.' He had to have yet another dig.

'Well,' I started. 'Royal Marines are supposed to know about ships and that, aren't they?' I said it loud enough for everyone at the table to hear, and in a tone that was challenging.

Everyone stopped talking.

John looked up. 'So what of it?' he said, in a very authoritative tone.

'You're just the sort of bloke that may be able to help me out on something that I have very often wondered about on board aircraft carriers,' I started on my assassination ploy. 'Especially as I'm a useless RAF bloke who don't know nowt about ships.'

'Well, if I can help you out, Mike,' John said with a rather important air. 'Fire away.'

'The thing is,' I started, 'on an aircraft carrier, there is a little piece that sticks out on the side of the flight deck.' Whilst I was asking the question. I had drawn a little diagram on a beer mat in front of me. The diagram was the simple outline of an aircraft carrier. 'Look there,' I pointed out the part of the angled flight deck that protruded over the side of the ship, more or less opposite the bridge. 'What's that little triangle for? Is that for the helicopters to land on?'

I was sitting in between John and Steve. Steve went to interrupt and tell me. But I quickly kicked him on the shin under the table. As the back of my head was facing John, I was able to look at Steve and quickly wink and grin. Fortunately, he got the message.

'No!' came the reply from John. John was full of his own importance as he knew the answer, and was able to tell a stupid Air Force wallah, that the triangle was not for helicopters to land on.

'That's what is called an angled flight deck for aircraft to come in to land on,' John started to explain.

By the time John had finished his explanation everyone else had cottoned onto what I was up to.

'Well I can't see that,' I came back, sounding as innocent as I could, 'how can an aircraft come in sideways to land on deck? It wouldn't have enough landing space.'

John went on to answer all the questions that I put forward. Each time, for one reason or another. I couldn't understand. By now the rest of John's mates were inwardly laughing at the prank I was playing, and were joining in with a question or two, egging John on to try and explain to me the pro's and con's of an Aircraft Carrier's angled flight deck. This practical joke went on for over half an hour. All the time John was gradually getting more and more annoyed at the questions that I would come back with. No matter what he tried to explain, I pretended I just couldn't see what he was trying to tell me. He must have thought I was most un-educated person there was and at the same time he must have thought what a load of useless prats the RAF were.

'No,' I started up again. 'I just can't see that an aircraft can come in, and land on an Aircraft Carrier sideways. I reckon you're trying to con me. You've got to have a length of runway for any aircraft to land on. I know your runways are shorter than the runways are on land. Because of that you put ropes across the deck for the aircraft to hook on.' I started to twist the noose a little tighter for John. 'Besides, I've seen pictures, and films of aircraft coming into land on aircraft carriers, and they always come in from the back. No John,' I closed the noose a little more. 'I reckon you're trying to take the piss out of me. To make out that an aircraft can come in to land on the side of the deck. You're taking the piss.'

Everything that John had been telling me and explained had been quite correct. I, and all the others around the table, were now finding it very hard to keep a straight face. I for one was determined to keep this hoax up for as long as I could. For one second John just sat there absolutely flabbergasted, that he couldn't explain, or get through to me what he was trying to say. Not knowing what else to say, he started on to me again. On and on he went. While he was gibbering on this time I thought I would do a little bit of doodling on a piece of paper. After he had finished gibbering – and he must have realised by now that he wasn't getting very far with this useless Airman I looked up, and said to him, passing him my little doodle. 'Is this what you mean by an angled flight deck?' My doodle had been a diagram of an angled flight deck, and in as much detail as I could muster.

'Mike Baker! You bastard. You bastard!' John shouted out loudly. Everyone was laughing like hell, at the ruse that I had kept going for such a long time.

'Well you said that you knew all about Aircraft Carriers and that. So I tried to test your knowledge,' I explained to him, laughing all the time.

By now the Tiger beer was in full flow, and another round was bought for all of us. 'Well I've been well and truly had,' said John. 'It'll teach me to keep my mouth shut in future.'

One of his mates looked up. 'You won't be such a know-all from now on will you. I'll tell you John, it's taken an Air Force bloke to teach you a lesson.'

'Mike Baker!' John started again. 'I've got to hand it to you. You've certainly taught me a lesson.' He caught hold of my hand and shook it. 'I still say you're a bastard though,' he grinned.

One particular day, after I had been in Singapore for several months, I had the chance to go to the Singapore Races. It all came about by my having an invitation from one of my work colleagues who was very interested in horse racing.

'Here Mike, ever been to a race meeting?' said Brian Foster.

'No, I can't say that I have,' I replied.

'Come with me on Thursday,' invited Brian. 'Are you off duty that day?'

'Yes, as a matter of fact, I finish at 08.00 that morning,' I replied. 'So I'll want to get some shut-eye before I even contemplate it.'

'That's alright. We needn't go till the afternoon anyway,' Brian said.

Not being very interested in horse racing, and not knowing the front end of a horse from the back, I wasn't really all that bothered. But I had heard that there was always a lovely atmosphere at race meetings, which made them worth a visit, if only once in a lifetime. For that reason, I decided to go.

'OK. I've never been to a race meeting before. So I'll come with you,' I said, not sounding very enthusiastic.

Brian came back, 'Great! I promise you'll enjoy it. There's a few English jockeys riding on Thursday. There's Lester Piggott and a few more.'

Brian did mention a few more jockeys by name, but not having any previous interest in horse racing, the names didn't mean a thing to me.

Thursday came. As usual, as every day is in Singapore it was hot and humid. We went to the Singapore Races, up the Bukit Timah Road by taxi. Brian took me into the grandstand and we sat down. There was the hustle and bustle around the course, especially around the stands. Without a doubt, there was an atmosphere about the place. The only way I can describe it was an air of excitement, and exhilaration. After a few minutes of looking around the area, Brian, who had been beside me all the time, pointed out different parts of the course and other things about which I knew nothing. He asked me, 'Mike, are you going to put a bet on any horses?'

'Now what would I know about betting? I told you before, I didn't have a clue about anything that's going on here.'

'Well, Lester Piggott is riding in all five races this afternoon,' Brian began. 'He's bound to win most races, if not all of them.'

'Oh yes,' I started to say but Brian interrupted. 'But of all the races he's riding in it's a cert he'll win the fourth one.'

'You reckon? How do you know that?' I questioned him.

'Honest. You put ten dollars on the fourth race. I guarantee he'll win it, if he don't win any other,' said Brian enthusiastically.

I was a little dubious about doing this, because ten dollars was a lot of money to me. It was nigh on twenty-five per cent of a week's wages, and I couldn't really afford it.

'You sure?' I questioned him again.

'Yeah, I'm sure. Come with me, and we'll put the bets on together,' said Brian, as he pulled me up to take me to the tote office, just above and behind us at the top of the stands. I followed Brian and I reluctantly parted with my ten dollars, which was put on Lester Piggott to win in the fourth race. We returned to our seats, and watched the first three races. Lester Piggott won the first. Then the second and the third race.

Finally, the fourth race came along. I was by now very excited, and was anticipating Lester to win his fourth race. Everyone at the race meeting was cheering on the horses that they had bet on. I as well as Brian, was cheering on Lester. As the horses came down the straight towards the finish line a roar went up, and grew even louder as the first horse passed the finish line. I myself didn't know whether Lester had come in first, second, or last. But Brian groaned as the first horse went past.

'Did he win?' I asked excitedly.

'No,' said Brian rather sheepishly. 'For some reason or other, he only came fourth.'

I felt absolutely demoralised as I too had been expecting Lester Piggott to win that race if not any other.

'Well, so much for your bloody certs,' I growled at Brian. 'I thought you said that of any race he was bound to win the fourth race was the one he would win,' I complained bitterly.

'That's right. He was. It was odds on that he should have,' said Brian. 'I just don't know what happened. I'm sorry Mike. But that's how it goes sometimes.' Brian was most apologetic, and at the same time I'm sure he felt somewhat embarrassed.

We watched the last race, although by now I had lost all interest in horse racing. The ironic thing was that the only race that I bet on was the only race that Lester Piggott lost in the whole afternoon. Although the afternoon was worth the experience, from that day on, I have never placed a bet on a horse. So much for certain forecasts.

There was one place in Singapore that always had a few prostitutes, and that was on the corner of Bras Basah Road and Bencoolen Street, not far from the Capital Cinema. They always used to hang around in the evenings in the dark alleyways of some shops that one would have to walk through to go to the cinema from the Britannia Club. I always noticed that these prostitutes were more or less at the end of their careers, which meant that they were not, shall we say, at their best as regards looks. It was no wonder that they would hang about in the dark alleyways. I would never even have contemplated going with them, due to watching the film about venereal diseases back at the Astra cinema at Changi. As I said earlier, the films were enough to put anyone off having sex with prostitutes, or any woman come to that.

Very often, I would be walking up Bras Basah Road, on the way to the cinema, or on my way to Orchard Road. I would be approached and propositioned.

'Good time Johnny?' One of the pros. would enquire.

Just for the fun and sheer devilment, I would fall in with their proposition and ask something like, 'Yeah! How much?'

The answer would be in the line of ten dollars all night, or five dollars for a short time. Any speciality was extra. I would enquire how much for everything, including all night.

'You want two girls Johnny?' would be the next question.

'Aye, that's not a bad idea,' would come my reply.

'Two girls, all night will cost you twenty-five dollars. Everything all in,' she would inform me.

It was then I would start to barter with them as regards the price.

'No, that's too much,' I would start. 'I'll give you five dollars,' or some other ridiculous price, knowing full well that the offer would be turned down. We would then start to barter. 'Oh no Johnny that's far too low. Even if it was for one girl,' one of the girls would say.

We would barter and haggle for quite a period of time. It was nothing to barter with them for up to a quarter of an hour or so. Eventually, after I had got them down to a price that was next to nothing and everything had been agreed, I would then come back with, 'Oh, I don't think I'll bother just now, girls,' then walk on my way. They would become outraged, and call me all the names under the sun, not only in English, but in their local tongue, because, while I had been haggling with them, several other would-be clients would have passed them by. What they didn't realise was that I was laughing quietly to myself, as I went on my way. I often thought that I had done some of their possible clients a service by haggling with the prostitutes while they passed by, and perhaps, saved them a dose.

Chapter Fifteen

Penang, and a Missed Opportunity

EVERY NOW AND THEN, after you had been in the services for a period of time you would be due for leave. In Singapore the Servicemen regardless of which Base they were in – be it at RAF Tengah, Seletar, or Changi – would have the opportunity of going to leave centres in Malaya at places like the Cameron Highlands, Fraser's Hill or an island just off the west coast of Malaya named Penang. I had a few chances of having a fortnight's leave, and decided, or was first persuaded, by other colleagues who had been there, to go to Sandycroft leave centre in Penang. The island was approximately five hundred miles north from Singapore.

From what I had been told, Sandycroft did everything for you. All meals, excursion trips (including a boat trip) bicycles and the like were free of charge. All you needed to take was your clothes and toiletries. The rest was found for you. This to me appeared to be a little exaggerated. But, from other things that had been said, I rather liked the sound of the place.

As soon as I knew that I had leave due to me, I booked a fortnight at Changi's Admin. Section for Sandycroft leave centre.

A day or so before I was due to go I went to get my leave pass and train warrant (ticket) and all other information that was forthcoming. The information given was quite considerable, and helped me greatly. I was given a ticket so that I could take the night sleeper train from Keppel Station in Singapore to Kuala Lumpur, and then go on to Perai Station. At Perai Station one had to get off and board a Ferry to go across the Straits of Penang. The train journey would take nearly twenty-four hours, leaving Singapore at 19.30 hours, and arriving at

Kuala Lumpur at approximately 06.00 next morning. We would then have to wait for about an hour or so for the next train to take passengers further north. This train was expected to pull away from Kuala Lumpur at about 08.00 hours. We would then travel until approximately 17.00 hours. arriving at Perai Station, and then take the ferry.

On boarding the ferry to go across the Straits, which only took about a quarter of an hour, we would be met by Sandycroft's leave centre staff, to be taken to Sandycroft. The leave centre was situated on the north-east corner of Penang Island.

According to others who had been to Penang already, Penang was supposed to be a little dryer than Singapore, but just as hot. In fact, it could be even warmer than Singers. Whereas in Singapore, your body tan was, shall we say, on the yellow side due to the humidity there, in Penang, your tan would be more copper in colour.

The day of my leave came along at last, and I got myself to Keppel Railway Station. The train was on a narrow gauge track, the gauge being only about two feet between each line. The steam engine had to pull approximately seven coaches, about a third of them being sleeper compartments. On boarding the train, every passenger who had booked a sleeper for the night's trip was taken to his allotted bunk. The bunks, or beds, were situated lengthways along the length of the carriage and each side of the gangway, the gangway being in the middle of the coach. There were two bunks, one on top of the other. Each bunk was kitted out with sheets, blanket and pillows, and had a curtain on the gangway side so that one could have some privacy. I had been lucky enough to have a bottom bunk.

The train left Singapore at 19.30 hours. It travelled slowly, towards the only bridge across to the Malayan mainland, known as the Causeway. We crossed the Straits of Johore and on the other side of the Causeway was the small town of Johore Bahru. From Johore Bahru the train wound its way through the jungle towards Kluang, and then on up to Kuala Lumpur. It was an uneventful journey. Although I had a bed to sleep on, I never slept all that well. The train arrived at KL at the correct time.

KL Station was a fascinating place. As I had at least an hour and half to wait, I decided to go and look around the area. The first thing that struck me was how English the whole structure of the station was. The roof had massive girders spanning it as if they were meant to take a great weight. I learnt later, that it had been part of the contract when the station was being built that the roof had to support at least three feet of snow. When I heard this, I laughed, because Kuala Lumpur is only approximately 225 miles north of the Equator Throughout its history. Kuala Lumpur had never seen snow. It's right in the middle of a tropical rainforest. I thought, typical British bureaucracy, and what a waste of money.

I went outside the station, and turned left, and walked to the end of the building, to where a road bridge went across the lines. I stood on the bridge looking back at the station. It was completely different outside to the Victorian styling inside. The whole of the building was like a palace, with minarets, turrets, and spires, and with Arabic-type arches in every direction. Opposite the main gateway to the station was another grand building, built in the same style as the station's perimeter, only this building was even more magnificent. It was the palace of all palaces. Except it wasn't a palace. It was the central HQ for the Malay railways.

It was soon time for me to get aboard the train for the last part of my journey. The train left on time, and before long it was chugging northwards. The train this time had carriages with seating compartments. The best way to describe these would be to liken them to the old Wild West carriages, where there was a single door to get out onto the end. Each end of the carriage had a small platform, with railings to catch hold of, and each side of the coach had iron steps to climb down when alighting from the train.

Finally after a long slow journey, past rice paddy-fields and rubber plantations, the train arrived at Perai station. As the train approached the station, I noticed that on each side of the track there were pineapples growing. It was the first time I had seen pineapples growing naturally. All the passengers who were due to alight for Penang got off. Some of them were military personnel. I didn't know where I had to go to get to the ferry, so I instinctively followed the rest of the passengers, struggling at the same time to carry my heavy baggage. They started to walk down a long trail, between the trees. The trail seemed to go on for ever but suddenly, we came out of the trees and onto a quay-side. At the quay-side was the ferry we had to aboard. After getting on board I went over to the other side of the ferry so that I could look at Penang Island. Unfortunately, I couldn't see Penang, because the ferry appeared to be docked up the mouth of a

River. All that could be seen on the other side of the river was the jungle. The ferry set off, down the mouth of the river and out into the Straits of Penang. The trip across the straits took about twenty minutes. This was a little longer than the information I had been given. After I got off the ferry I stood looking around to see where I had to report. A WVS woman approached me, enquiring if I was on my way to Sandycroft. She was dressed in a grey/green uniform, with a hat with the Women's Voluntary Service cap badge attached to it. I said that I was for Sandycroft. She asked for my name, and which camp I had come from. After she had ticked me off her list, she told me to board a bus that was parked nearby. The journey to Sandycroft leave centre didn't take very long, approximately a half hour. I was delighted at this, because I was beginning to feel absolutely knackered, due to not sleeping all that well the night before on the train. I was booked in with the rest of the airmen who had come in the coach with me. We were taken to our sleeping quarters by one of the members of the staff, our quarters being built along the same lines as the wooden billets at RAF Bridgnorth. The only difference being that there were no windows, only shutters, and each bed had a mosquito net hanging over it. We were advised to use the nets, because the mossies were that little bit bigger, and could, if we were bitten, leave a nice mark on the body. Apart from that, the bite could cause a lot of irritation for days afterwards, or worse, possibly give you malaria.

It was dark by now. As most of us had been up for over twenty four hours, and not being able to sleep for one reason or other, we were ready to take the advice that had been freely given. We settled down, under our mosquito nets, and were all soon asleep.

Next morning, on our way to get breakfast, a lot of us were interested to see what Penang and the leave centre were like. From what I could see Sandycroft leave centre was situated just outside a village called Tanjong Bungah, and on the edge of a lovely tropical beach. Lining the beach was nothing but coconut trees, and the inland consisted of nothing less than lush jungle. The beach was lovely, with soft, fine sand, and the sea was a lovely turquoise blue (similar to Changi beach). It had a nice warm temperature of at least eighty degrees, just like getting into a warm bath back home in Blighty.

The grounds of the leave centre had a parkland environment, with the road and buildings lined with colourful shrubs, coconut trees, and a tree called flame of the jungle. During part of the year, this would

come out in a massive bloom of flame red flowers, and not much of
the greenery could be seen, hence its name.

We had been requested to assemble in the lounge at ten a.m. while
we were booking in the night before. This was a reasonable request
because it gave everyone a chance to get a good night's sleep, and
breakfast before the briefing in the lounge. All the new arrivals sat in
the lounge just before ten, after having a good old English breakfast of
egg, bacon, fried bread, and baked beans. Most of us had a drink in
our hands, like a cup of tea, or coffee, and were generally chatting
amongst ourselves whilst we waited for the briefing, asking each other
what they had seen, or what the place was like.

Through one of the several doors came a WVS woman holding several
sheets of paper. As she sat down in one of the wicker chairs that was in the
lounge she said a cheerful 'Good morning' and put her paperwork on the
table in front of her. She was a middle-aged woman, around forty-five
years of age, roughly five foot nine, tall and slender, with greying hair.

'Gentlemen,' she said. 'Would you all please sit around, so that I
can double-check that you are all here.'

She went through all of our names, and as each name was called out
the named person would answer. After she had completed the roll call,
she started, 'Well, gentlemen. Welcome to Sandycroft leave centre.
I'm sure that you will enjoy your leave here.'

A few around answered meekly, 'Thank you'.

She then started again with a smile on her face. 'My name is Joyce
Alison. Joyce to you.' She paused for her introduction to be digested,
and then went on. 'As some of you will know, or may not know
Sandycroft is not a military establishment as such. What I mean by
that, is that although it is a leave centre for military personnel, it is run
in conjunction with the Women's Voluntary Service, and the NAAFI.
There are no military rules here. You will be treated like any civilian
on holiday. So you can come and go just as you please.'

A cheer went up from most of us at the last statement. Joyce then
added, after the cheer had died down. 'If you want to take it easy and
just laze around on the beach, then please be free to do so. You don't
have to engage in anything, if you don't want to.'

'That's for me!' said one individual.

'Now let me tell you what there is to do in Sandycroft, and the
excursions that are held for you to go on.' She paused, then added,
'That is, if you want to go on them, of course.'

She then went on to say that there were bicycles for anyone that
wished to go for a cycle up the coast; rowing boats and fishing tackle
for those who wanted to go sea fishing. Also, for those who were
keep-fit fanatics, there was a gymnasium, and tennis courts. She also
told us what the local people were like, especially for those of us who
had come from further afield than Singapore. It was also a popular
place for RAF chaps based right out in the middle of the Indian Ocean
at a place called Gan Island. (RAF Gan) Gan Island being one of the
many islands in the Maldives.

'For those of you who want to go on an island coach tour or a
special boat trip,' she added as an after thought, 'we even have a
motor-boat that will take at least twenty persons around the island.'
She grinned at those of us who were chuckling at her last comment.
'But please let us know that you wish to come at least twenty-four
hours before she finished. 'Finally!' Joyce said. 'If anyone has anything
that they want to know, please, please do not be afraid to ask for
advice from any of the staff here.'

Once again, Joyce came back as if she'd forgotten to say something.
'One other thing, and this is the best thing of all.' She stood up,
putting out hands to us and saying proudly. 'No matter what you
decide to do – go on the motor-boat trip or the coach tour – no
matter what it is you decide to do, it won't cost you a single cent,
because everything is laid on free of charge.'

A loud cheer went up.

I had at least a fortnight to spend at Sandycroft, so I decided to spend
the first couple of days quietly in and around the leave centre, then perhaps go on a few of the excursions, starting off with a bike, since they
were free. My first excursion on a bike was up the Coastal Road. I
went off, with a friend I had made whilst at Sandycroft. Steve Meadows
was up from RAF Tengah, and was in the same trade as I, so it was
characteristic for us to muck in together. We started off up the narrow
main road, only to find that the road hugged the coast more than we
had anticipated. It wound and twisted, uphill and down dale and the
temperature was well up in the nineties. What beautiful scenery we
were to see that afternoon neither of us would ever be likely to forget.
Fortunately, I had a thirty-five millimetre camera with me.

'Bloody hell,' said Steve. 'I can't go much further in this sweltering
heat.'

'Hells bells, Steve,' I came back. 'We've only just started, and you're bloody whining.'

'I know. But I'm not used to cycling, especially in this heat,' moaned Steve.

'Come on. If you look up the road you can see it goes into some trees that will give us some shade,' I pointed further up the road. 'Let's get there, and then we'll stop for a drink.'

We cycled up to the trees which shaded the road. We stopped, and sat at the side of the road for a breather, and took a swig of water that we had brought with us. While Steve sat wiping his face and arms, I decided to take a look through the trees. What I saw made me certain that I was going to go on up the road.

I looked down to see what I thought was the most beautiful sight that I had ever seen in my life. Below was a small bay, with large boulders in the sea, the water a light emerald green, lapping at the sand. The bay was lined with palm trees with jungle spreading inland.

'Steve,' I cried out. 'Come and see this view. It's absolutely fabulous.'

Steve came over slowly, as if only to keep me happy. I was in the process of taking a photograph when he reached me.

'That's bloody beautiful. Absolutely fantastic!' cried Steve, as he looked down at this tropical paradise. 'I always dreamed of seeing places like this, but never thought I'd see anything like it,' said Steve.

'Yeah, it is nice isn't it,' I agreed. 'Come on. I'm not stopping now, or turning back. Let's go on. You with me ?' I asked.

'If this is only the beginning of what's on further,' said Steve. 'Then I'm with you Mike'.

Steve seemed to have more vitality in him now, and was as enthusiastic about going on as I was. At each bend we went round we came to more bays, as fantastic as the first. We seemed to be the only ones around. All that could be heard was the sound of the sea, and the jungle. Every now and then we would pass an isolated *Kampong* (village). We cycled on and on and eventually we came across an Army camp right on a point of land. Outside the camp were some English Army wallahs.

'I wonder how far we have come,' said Steve.

'Aye, I wonder,' I echoed.

'Let's ask those Army blokes over there by the gate,' said Steve, as he made his way over to them he stopped by the gates of the barracks.

'Hey mate, any idea where we bloody well are?' asked Steve, as I arrived beside him.

'Yeah,' said the Army chap, questioningly. 'Why?'

'Because we've cycled, and cycled for miles, and we ain't got a clue where we are,' said Steve in an assertive manner.

'What mob are you two in?' asked the Army chap.

There was an antagonistic air about this Army chap that gave me the impression that we were not going to get very far with him. 'We're in the RAF,' I came in. 'Were on leave at Sandycroft, and all we want to know is where we are. That's all, nothing else.'

The soldier gave some comment rather like 'Tough!'

'Come on Steve, we're not going to get anywhere with this idiot,' I said, as I pushed off on the bike. Steve followed.

We cycled on down round the corner, and onto a long straight piece of road. About a quarter of mile further on we came to a village called Batu Feringghi and decided to go through it, see what was around the distant corner. Then turn around and make for home. We cycled through the village. Each side of the road was flat, and sandy. Set back amongst the multitude of coconut trees were many *Kampongs* all on stilts, with their typical banana and palm leaf roofs. Occasionally, the roofs were made up of corrugated sheets. The ground around each was meticulously clean. The village seemed to be at peace with itself. As we cycled through some of the locals would wave out and express a form of greeting, all with a smile on their faces. As we went around the corner, we looked back along the coast. There was the most magnificent beach one could want to see. It went right back to the point where the Army barracks were and I reckoned that the beach must have been at least a mile long. We decided that before we made back for home we both deserved a swim in the sea to cool down. Both of us by now were feeling the effects of our long, arduous cycle ride and were sweating tremendously.

'I ain't brought anything to swim in,' said Steve.

'Tough! So what,' I put my hands out, in exasperation. 'Just take it all off,' I said.

Before he had time to answer I was running down the beach towards the water. I dived into the lovely warm, yet refreshing, water. Steve and I swam and generally played about in the water for a little time, then came out of the water, and lay on some grass that we found at the edge of the beach. It took about an half hour for us to dry off in the sun before we set off back to Sandycroft. By the time we had returned to Sandycroft both of us were feeling the benefits of our afternoon's expedition. We were both saddle-sore, and absolutely exhausted. It would take at least a day to recuperate.

Another day I was sitting in the gardens under the shade of some of the wonderful trees, and just above the sea wall. The gardens were approximately ten feet above the beach, with a set of steps every few yards along for anyone who wished to go into the sea, or walk to the beach. As usual it was a lovely balmy afternoon. All around one could hear the sounds of the jungle; the screeching of monkeys, as they fought amongst themselves for food or for supremacy over the rest of the pack; the barely audible hissing of the different insects in the background; the croaking of bull-frogs somewhere in the dampness of the trees.

I was sat on a wooden bench-like seat, with another similar seat situated on the other side of the table. On the table was a nice ice-cool glass of Tiger beer. I felt it was sheer bliss, with not a worry on my mind. Down below on the beach, I watched a little girl, no more than five or six years of age, playing at the water's edge. The water was lapping her tiny feet. As I sipped my beer, I watched the little girl playing her innocent game as a few people were walked past her, and on along the beach. Everything was so peacefully quiet, it was paradise.

As I looked along the wall, I could see one of the locals who was employed by Sandycroft to act as a life-guard. He was sitting on an old dining room chair by the sea wall, pushing his chair backwards with his feet against the wall. He had on his head a Chinese straw coolie hat, which was sloped over his face to shield his eyes. He didn't seem to have a care in the world and appeared to be asleep. This peaceful bliss went on for quite a while when all of a sudden, out of the corner of my eye, I saw the life-guard jump down the ten-foot drop of the sea wall, and chase towards the little girl. She was squatting down on the water's edge with a stick about twelve inches long, and prodding the water's edge. The life-guard ran to her, literally caught hold of her, and manually threw her over his shoulders up the beach. The little girl crashed to the ground, and started to cry. I looked in absolute astonishment that a man could literally throw a baby ten feet and not give a hoot as to how she fell. How dare he treat a small girl like that?

I was half way out of my seat with anger when I noticed that the life-guard had taken the stick away from the little girl and was beating the hell out of the water.

After a few beatings of the water, I noticed that the life-guard was now trying to lift something out of the water with the stick from the area where he had been thrashing away. Hooked over the stick was a sea snake. It was about eighteen inches long. These snakes can kill, and once bitten, a person doesn't have very long to live. They say about ten minutes. I can only assume from what I saw that day that the little girl had found the sea snake as it swam along the water's edge and had started to play with it by prodding it with the stick she had in her hand. Obviously, she was too young to realise what danger she had been in. Fortunately for her, the life-guard had seen what she was doing and rescued her from a bite, and near certain death.

Although it was common knowledge that this part of the world was full of sea snakes and jelly fish, at certain times of the year, I had never really taken much notice of the fact. After seeing that incident, I never went into the sea again in that part of the country; I always went into a swimming-pool. It certainly warned me as to what could happen.

The day came when I went ahead and booked up for the sightseeing tour of the island. It was a complete afternoon tour by coach. We were told that if we wanted to have a swim, it was advisable to take some swimwear. We set off, with a full coach. We were told that we would be seeing Kek Lok Si Temple – which was a Buddhist temple – a snake temple, and several other places that may be of interest to us, most of which would be in the jungle. I had a rather open mind as to the snake temple, because I wasn't all that keen on snakes and had a slight phobia about them, but was looking forward to the other places of interest.

I teamed up with Steve again. In actual fact, we seemed to go around together from the first day we met at Sandycroft. As usual it was a warm day, as every day was. The coach left Sandycroft and followed the road that Steve and I had taken towards Batu Feringghi a few days before on our bicycles. About ten minutes from Sandycroft the coach took a left-hand turn and started to wind its way up a jungle road. On each side of us were trees that completely covered the road, so that hardly any sunshine came through. The road was wet, and one could hear all the life sounds of the jungle outside. After a further ten minutes, the coach took a right-hand turn, and continued up a steep hill. At the top the coach stopped to let all the passengers out. We walked a little way up a tarmac path, which led up to the top of the hill. As we all came to the rim of the hill a large reservoir came in sight below us. Its wall, and towers were all painted white. The water was crystal clear, and gave off a reflection of the sky – a brilliant blue colour. With the surrounding hills covered in trees, the green and white sight of the reservoir was spectacular. This was the Guillemuir Reservoir. After several of us had taken photographs, we were on our way again.

As we followed the road, which most of the time was jungle green, with the occasional *Kampong*, we went past an Army barracks, known as Minden Barracks. After passing Minden Barracks, a few miles on the coach took off to the right, down an old dirt track for about two hundred yards. The coach stopped and we were ushered off. The time was three o'clock in the afternoon. By now, most of us were feeling a little worse for the heat, bearing in mind that the coach had no air conditioning. We were told that, if we had brought our swimming costumes and we cared to walk down a small single track which was pointed out to us about two hundred yards on, we would find a small freshwater pool, and a waterfall. We were told that the water came from the top of Penang Hill and we could spend an hour there before the coach was due to start off to our next destination.

'Come on Mike, let's be first there,' said Steve. 'I'm sweating cobblers.' Steve's shirt at the back by now, as everyone else's, was absolutely soaking wet from perspiration.

'Race you there, Steve,' I cried. We both started to run down the track, with Steve closely behind me. We left everyone else behind. We came to the small pool approximately twenty feet wide, and it was ten feet to the back of the pool, and was approximately eight to ten feet in depth. At the back of the pool was a waterfall which dropped approximately seven to ten feet into the pool. The whole of it was surrounded by rocks and boulders. By using the boulders at the side, one could climb to the top of the waterfall.

As I had my swimming trunks on already under my shorts, I was undressed before one could blink. It was so hot, I was in a hurry to get to the top of the waterfall to dive in that nice cool water. I ran towards the boulders at the side of the pool, shouting out to Steve, 'Come on Steve, I thought you were in a hurry.'

By the time I had climbed to the top of the waterfall most of the others had arrived from the coach. There was I, and in front of me was a nice little audience. I could show them how a dive should be done. I launched myself off a small rock at the side of the waterfall. The water below looked so enticing. I hit the pool below. Immediately, panic struck me, I came out of the water so fast. It was like a penguin jumping out of the water onto an ice floe in the Antarctic.

'Ah-h-h-h-h-h-h-h!' I screamed out, as I came out of the water. 'That water is bloody cold.' Everyone was laughing at my predicament. Next second, another great splash came from the pool. It was Steve, who had decided not to dive, but to do a bomb burst. A few of the spectators got soaked through from his massive splash. Steve was out of the water, as fast as I had been.

'Bleeding hell!' he swore as he came out of the water. 'I wondered why you came out of that pool so fast,' said Steve. 'I bloody well know now.' Then to all the others he announced, 'You all go in that water at your own peril. It's bloody well perishing in there.'

Pam, the WVS woman who was with us as our tour courier, was stood back laughing so much that tears were rolling down her cheeks. When I saw her laughing at both of us I said to her, 'You rotten sod. You knew it was this cold. But you didn't tell us, did you.'

She started to laugh even more after I spoke to her. After she had calmed down, and still with a little chuckle in her voice, she said, 'Oh Mike, if you had seen your face as you came out of that water.' She started to laugh again.

'Come on,' cried Steve. 'Let's get her, and see how she likes the water.' He and I, and a couple of the other fellows ran after her, and grabbed hold of her by her arms, as she made to run off. They manhandled her to the water's edge. She was by now screaming her head off. 'No, no, let me down! You can't do this. I shall get all my clothes wet, and this is all I've got on.'

'Tough!' came back the answer from one of her captors.

Steve winked at all of us who had hold of her, and grinned.

'Come on, Mike. She was laughing at you and your misadventure. Let's see how she likes it.'

Pam cried out, 'No, you can't do this to me,' as four of us caught hold of her legs and arms.

'Right. On the count of three. Let go!' shouted Steve.

'One!' as we swung her back and forth.

'Two!' as she was swung back again.

'Three-e-e-e!' as she was swung for the last time, and out towards the water.

Pam screamed and screamed.

As she went forward. I, and another fellow let go of her legs, whilst Steve, and his partner hung on to her so that she was swung around away from the water.

As she was lowered to the ground she cursed us all, at the same time she was laughing. 'You rotten sods.'

'You thought you were going in, didn't you ?' said one of the fellas who had been standing by watching.

'You're rotten, the lot of you,' she said laughing.

Now that we all knew about the water's temperature, everyone that had decided to get into the water entered it with a little more caution. The pool was nice and cool, once one had got used to the temperature, but to go in like Steve and I had, was a little bit too much for the system to take.

The hour passed, and then we were on our way again. The next stop being the snake temple, and then on to Kek Lok Si Temple. We spent about half an hour in the snake temple. As one can imagine, there were snakes hanging around the altar on small sticks or branches. The branches were placed in a small vase, and had hens' eggs placed at the bottom of the branches. The whole of the area smelt of the burning of joss sticks. The incense that burnt off the joss sticks kept the snakes doped, so that they were drowsy all the time whilst visitors were there. Once the visitors had gone the joss sticks would, I suppose, be removed so that the snakes would come out of their stupor and feed themselves on the hens' eggs below.

After looking at the green snakes (pit vipers) on the altar, we were ushered into a small room where photographers would adorn you with these snakes. They would be placed in your hand, around your neck and over your head. Then they would take a photo of you holding these pit vipers. Needless to say, I didn't bother.

Outside the temple itself, and to the right of it, were some large cages. Inside these were some of the biggest pythons that I had ever seen in my life. One had apparently just been fed with a large rabbit, or something of that size. Every python had to be fed with a live animal, so that it could kill its own prey by constricting it (squeezing it to death). It would not accept a dead carcass.

From the snake temple the coach went onto Kek Lok Si Temple, sometimes called the Temple of Paradise. This was the most marvellous building I had ever seen. Temple of Paradise was the right name for it as it was the most colourful temple one could imagine. It was the largest Buddhist temple complex in the whole of South-east Asia. The pagoda was around ninety to a hundred feet tall. It was often known as the Tower of a million Buddhas, due to the fact there are so many statues and tiles with Buddhas painted on them. The pagoda has seven storeys of mixed Chinese, Thai, and Burmese architecture and craftsmanship. The bottom half of the pagoda contained Chinese architecture, while the middle part contained Thai architecture, and the top part was of Burmese architecture. The first half of the pagoda on the outside was painted white with ornate paintings; and the top floor and spire were painted in brilliant gold. The three colourful Halls of the Great which were situated at the side of the pagoda, had a statue of one Buddha, or another. Invariably the statues were painted in gold, and were nearly as big as the halls that housed them.

From there, we were taken to the bottom of Penang Hill. The summit of the hill was approximately 2,460 feet above sea level. To get up to the top of the hill one had to ride up on the only funicular railway. Again, the only one in the whole of South-east Asia. The ride was so long that it took at least half an hour to reach the top, and even then, one had to change trains, or cable-car as it was, half way up the hill. The trains were run by using two cable cars, attached to a thick cable, which passed through pulleys. As one went up, so the other came down. The views from the top were, however, really worth the trip. The panorama of the whole of Penang, and some of the coast of the Malayan mainland, was out of this world. One could see the whole of Georgetown, plus the States of Wellesley, Kedah, and Perak across the water. The air was cool and fresh, which made a change from the hot and humid air at the bottom of the Hill. We spent at least an hour up on the top of Penang Hill, before everyone on the coach party came back down. We returned the same way as we went up since it was the only way to get to the top, as there were no roads up to the summit. The island tour was now over, and had been very enjoyable. By the time the coach got back to Sandycroft everyone was glad to strip off and have a shower.

The holiday in Penang was to be one that I would never forget. In fact, I enjoyed Penang so much I went there at every opportunity. In all, I must have gone up there on at least three or four occasions.

For a number of months, I had become very friendly with a American air crew who used to fly into Changi every couple of weeks. The aircraft that they flew in was the giant C74 Globemaster belonging to Military Air Transport Systems. (MATS) The aircraft was so big that it would easily take into its fuselage two double-decker buses. The four engines looked so small in comparison to the fuselage it looked as if the engines could not power the aircraft along the runway, let alone fly it.

I came to meet one of the airmen one night, as I happened to be on duty at the Com-cen. A knock came on the sliding service hatch, at around 01.00 hours. The sliding door was situated in a hole in the wall beside the main door. On my opening the hatch door, an American airman asked if he could send a message to his base, just on the outskirts of Tokyo. After I had seen his certification he was invited inside the Com-cen – which was normally against regulations – so that he could write out his message in the light. As he came in through the door he introduced himself as Craig. He was the Quatermaster Sergeant on board the Globemaster, that had recently landed at Changi. He offered each one of us on duty a cigarette, called a Paramount. It was the largest cigarette that I had ever seen. It must have been at least four inches long, and with the filter tip added, at least five inches. One of the lads asked where he had got the cigarettes from. He replied that it was the normal service issue. When we smoked the cigarette, each one of us stated how nice and smooth it was.

'It's the best cigarette that I've ever smoked,' I remarked.

After the Quatermaster Sergeant had written his message and it had been sent off, he started to ask about the local activities which were around the camp, also, what Singapore was like. We more or less told him that there was the Malcolm Club and anything else that he might have been interested in. As he was a Sergeant, there was also the Sergeants' Mess but he didn't want to know anything about rank.

'I'm not one for rank, you guys. When I'm off duty, which I shall be for a few days here, I'm no different than you, he started. 'And by the way, my name's Craig. Not Sergeant. OK?'

Fortunately, the night was rather a quiet night as far as work was concerned, so we all sat around the office generally talking, asking Craig this and that and about the USAAF. I discovered that I took to Craig well, and, fortunately for me, he seemed to take to me.

As I was off duty for the next two days, after I had finished at 08.00 hours my time was my own. I said to Craig, 'So you want to see what Singers is like?'

His reply was, of course, in the affirmative, so I made arrangements to take him downtown, later on in the afternoon after I'd had some shut-eye, once I had come off duty. Craig seemed to be really pleased with the offer, and made his way back to the quarters that he had been given, along with the rest of his mates on board the C74.

That afternoon, I met Craig, as arranged. I asked him how he wanted to travel, by bus or taxi.

'Mike, I want to experience everything that you have to offer. So you do whatever what you usually do,' he said in his American drawl.

'Right,' I said. 'It will be by bus going into town, and then by pick-up taxi back home.'

That afternoon was quite an experience for Craig, who appeared to enjoy every moment of his visit to the city. It was, of course obvious that we went to the Britannia Club to start with.

On the following day, I took him back downtown to show him some other attractions. For instance, Tiger Balm Gardens, Change Alley and one of the 'Worlds,' He took a liking to Bugis Street, during the evening, especially the 'girls' there. He wouldn't believe me at first, when I tried to explain to him what they were.

I did find one thing that Craig did not like doing much and that was to walk. He would sooner get a taxi. Even if it was only for approximately a hundred and fifty to two hundred yards.

Over the two days that we were together we got on exceptionally well, and a good friendship was born. Every time that Craig landed at Changi after that he would look me up, whether it be at Com-cen Changi, block 144, or at the swimming pool. It was nothing for Craig to come to the billet, and find me fast asleep in my pit after coming off night duty. As time went on, Craig used to tell me about his home base at Tachikawa, which was just twenty-two miles outside Tokyo. I'd also got to know the rest of the American crew who were great guys. Another thing that I found out in the early days was that they earned as much in a day, on subsistence, as I did, on a fortnight's wages. They were picking up eighty-two dollars a day subsistence, plus their normal pay. All I was picking up was eighty-four as wages for the whole fortnight. How I envied them. As the months went by, it became clear to them that I would be leaving Singapore soon to become demobbed.

'Why don't you come with us to Tachikawa, Mick,' said Craig.

'Oh, I'd love to do that. But you know as well as I do, I just can't afford to do it,' I replied.

'Don't worry about the money side. You don't have to bring a dime. All your bedding, money, and travel will be on us. All you gotta do is bring yourself,' was the answer.

'Lads,' I said as there were more airmen than Craig there at the time when the subject was raised. 'I love the thought. I really do. But I haven't any leave left.'

'Just try and get some leave Mick. If you can get it, just think, it will be Manila, in the Philippines for five days. Then fly from there to Tachikawa, twenty-two miles outside Tokyo for another five days or so. Your bed, finances, and flight, all found – all on the compliments of the United States of America,' said Craig.

'And us,' added another of the crew, laughing.

'Come on Mike. Just try and see if you can get some leave by the time we come back from our next round trip,' persuaded Craig. They were all trying to coax me to make a effort to come with them on the next trip.

'OK, OK,' lifting my hands in the air, as if in surrender. 'I'll try, and see what I can do. But I warn you, don't expect miracles. I don't belong to USAF. I'm in the British Royal Air Force you know. They think different to you,' I explained.

After they had taken off for Manila, I thought about their invitation. It was, without doubt, a chance in a lifetime. So I decided to see what could be done about getting additional leave. After all, nothing ventured, nothing gained.

The first thing was to go to see the Warrant Officer at the Comcen. WO Davies was getting near to his retirement from the RAF. He was a man who had a rather fatherly disposition, a man that one could go to with any problems. He very often managed to sort the problems out. He was a real gent. I went into see him, on the next occasion I happened to be on duty. I tapped on his door.

'Come in,' he ordered.

As one went in the first thing that sprang to your notice was his distinctive white hair.

'Yes Baker? What can I do for you?' he asked.

'Sir, I don't know whether you can help me but I have a chance of a lifetime of going to the Philippines and Japan,' I started.

'Have you by God!' He looked at me in some sort of surprise. 'Can I come with you,' he said jokingly.

'I'd be glad to see you with me,' I replied. 'The only trouble is that I have no leave left, until I go home on disembarkation leave.'

'Alright Baker, I'll see what can be done,' he smiled. 'But I warn you, don't expect too much to come from it,' he finished.

'Sir, I'm quite happy to forgo my disembarkation leave to go there. As I said, it's a trip of a lifetime, and I may never get the chance again of going to Japan,' I finished.

'It's alright, Baker. If I were in your shoes, I'd want to do the same.' WO Davies could see my willingness to give everything else up just to go. 'As I said, I'll see what I can do for you.'

With that I left his office.

A few days later, I was called in to see the Flight Lieutenant Milne, Officer In Command Com-cen Changi.

I walked into his office as I was in camp I came to attention, and saluted him. 'I believe you wish to see me, sir?' I asked.

'Yes Baker. What's this I hear about you wanting to go with an American Aircrew of a Globemaster to visit the Philippines and Japan,' he questioned me.

'That's correct, sir. As you know there are two or three Yankee Globemasters, that come in here every week,' I began.

'Yes, go on,' the Officer nodded.

'Well, sir, I have become very friendly with one of the crews. Every fortnight when they come into Changi we all go out together downtown. They've given me the chance to fly to Manila and Tachikawa, and then fly back here with them,' I explained.

'That's all very well, Baker. But what about money and the guarantee of a flight back here?' The Flight Lieutenant queried.

'The money side doesn't come into it, sir. They know I'm a National Serviceman, and haven't much money. In their own words sir. I don't have to take a dime,' I explained.

'Yes that's all very well, Baker. But what if the aircraft, or crew have their flights changed to the USA, or whatever? What would you do if you were in Japan? You wouldn't have any way of getting back would you Baker?'

He had started to dampen my enthusiasm. I had this feeling that the Establishment were not going to let me go. But I still wanted to.

'I don't think that will be any problem, sir. I'm sure the crew that I'm going with would make certain I got back alright, sir.' I tried to justify my trip. 'I've known the crew for quite some months, sir. I'd trust them with my life.'

The Flight Lieutenant then changed the subject. 'I also understand that you have no leave left, Baker?'

'That's right, sir,' I answered quietly.

'Well, if you have no leave, how can you expect to go on a trip of this nature?' He asked.

'I've thought of that as well, sir,' I started.

'Oh, you have,' said the Flight Lieutenant, stretching his arms above his head, and clasping his fingers together.

'Yes sir, I know I'm due for disembarkation leave, when I go home to Blighty, just before I get demobbed,' I explained.

'Go on!' answered the Officer.

'Sir, I have a once in a lifetime chance of seeing Japan. I doubt if I shall ever get the chance again. I'm willing to even give up all the rest of my leave that I'm due for,' I implored. 'Even if it means going back, and having no leave whatsoever, until I'm actually demobbed.'

'You really are set on going, aren't you, Baker?' He said in a rather sorrowful tone. 'I can't really blame you for that. As you say, it is a chance of a lifetime. I'd like to go as much as you. Unfortunately, Baker, it's not in my hands to decide. It has already been decided for me. I'm sorry – and I mean it personally – I'm sorry. But I have been ordered to tell you that you will not be allowed to go.' The Flight Lieutenant sounded really sorry for me.

I was upset at not being allowed permission, but was not entirely surprised at the verdict. It was a missed opportunity, but that was fate. I had to accept it. I didn't like it, but that was it. What a bastard – a real golden opportunity missed.

Chapter Sixteen

Demob

I HAD BEEN in Singapore for eighteen months. Time was getting near for me to go home, and become demobbed from Her Majesty's Royal Air Force. Because I was enjoying myself at Changi so much I didn't want to leave Singapore. Fortunately, through a friend of a friend, I had been given the chance to stay in Changi, for just a little longer.

It came about that a Warrant Officer in charge of administration, was a friend of a Flight Sergeant whom I was very friendly with, due to a mate of mine, John, going out with his daughter. It's a little complicated, so I won't go into too much detail, but a few months earlier. I had been approached at a families party, to which I had been invited. Did I wish to go home on the *MV Nevasa*? This ship was going to be the very last troopship to be used by the armed services from Singapore. My reply was that I didn't wish to due to the fact that:

a   I wanted to stay in Singapore for as long as I could.
b   I wasn't a very good sailor, and,
c   I would have liked, if possible, to go home in the very latest aircraft, which was at that time, the De Havilland Comet 4C.

My wishes had been fulfilled. So much so, that I had been kept back in Singapore for a further couple of months. Which made me almost go over my stint of two years. The official excuse being the outbreak of hostilities in Laos.

Eventually, it was made known to me that I couldn't stay any longer and had to go home to be demobbed. On one of the days of my last week at work. I was called into see Flight Lieutenant Milne o/i/c Com-cen Changi. He asked me if I wanted to go home, to which my reply was very much in the negative.

'Have you thought any more of signing on, Baker?' he asked me, after I had said that I didn't want to go home.

To be truthful I was now in a bit of a quandary because I found that I was enjoying the service life, and was most definitely tempted to sign on for a few more years in the RAF. But, because I had been so indoctrinated into the General Post Office way of thinking, I could not see anything else but Post Office.

'No, thank you sir. I've had wonderful time here. But I think my future lies with the GPO.' Then I added, and I meant every word of it, 'but, if I find that I can't cope with civilian life again, then you will certainly be seeing me back.'

'Well Baker, I'm sorry that you're going. Your reports are very good. You've done everything that has been expected of you. I thank you for that,' said Flight Lieutenant Milne. He offered his hand in a handshake, which I returned with no hesitation. As we were shaking hands he brought up the subject of my trip to Japan.

'I'm sorry that you didn't make it to Japan the other month. I'd love to have seen you go, but as I said, it was out of my hands.'

'That's alright sir, but it was a chance in a lifetime, wasn't it?' I replied.

'Yes! It was,' he admitted. 'It's a place that I would love to see myself.'

We broke our handshake and saluted each other. Then I turned about, and marched out of his office.

Two of my mates in the billet were also due to go home the same day as I, their names being Steve Jacobs and Bob Stansted.

'What about painting the town red, Mike, on our last day before leaving for Blighty?' asked Steve, a week or so before we were due to go home.

'No, not for me, my old mates.' I said in reply. 'I've got nothing to celebrate. I don't want to go home. I could live out here with no trouble at all for the rest of my life. I love the country, the climate, and everything that goes on here.'

I had by now really fallen in love with the country of Singapore and

I really wasn't looking forward to leaving.

'Well, Bob and I are,' came back Steve. 'We're going to hire a car, go downtown, (Singapore,) in our best tuxedos, and really live it up.'

'I couldn't afford that sort of life, you know that,' I said. 'Christ, it'll cost a bomb.'

'So what?' said Bob, as he came in on the conversation. 'We're not only going to hire a car, but we're going to pick up a couple of birds, and have a gorgeous day out. Bugger the expense.'

'Well, thanks for the offer. But not for me,' I replied. 'I just can't see myself painting the town red. Especially on the money I get. It's alright for you full-timers. You've got the money.'

The day came for us to start our packing to go home. Steve and Bob had done their packing the day before, because they had arranged their day out. I had been persuaded to have a small party at the Chalet Club, which was situated down by the Pagar (playing fields) and the swimming pool. It was normally the custom, if one so wished, for everyone who knew a person going back to Blighty, to be at his or her party. The party was always called a boat party. If you were not there (unless you were on duty, or the like) it was taken as an insult. At the Chalet Club, which was part of the NAAFI, everyone I knew was there. From mates of old, to the newest recruit that had come out the day or so before. Here was I about to go, and him, the new recruit, just arriving. The lucky bastard. I was so envious of him. There were WRAFs from the Flight Operations room. Flight Operations being the office next to Com-cen Changi. There were also some WRAF nurses whom I knew from the hospital. Everybody who knew Mike Baker was there. I was expecting approximately a hundred or so people at my boat party, before the end of the evening. Some would stay the whole evening and drink with me. Some would come just to say good-bye and then go on their way. Needless to say, I didn't pay for very much that evening. It's just as well because there was no way that I could have afforded to buy everyone a drink. Still, it was the custom for everyone to buy the poor brat that was going home a last drink. I remember being escorted to the bar, when I first arrived. 'What would you like, Mike?' said one of my mates from the billet. 'Expense is no problem. It's your party,' he said.

'I'll ha-a-a-ve . . .' I said lingering as I looked at the different bottles behind the bar. Then I saw something that I hadn't seen for nearly two years. 'That bottle of Davenport Cider, please,' It was only a small bottle, but I had to have it. I hadn't tasted any cider for a long time, and it looked really appetising in the bottle.

I turned to go and sit down. It was then that realized I was being beckoned and called out to from across the floor where two WRAFs were sitting with a few more of my friends. 'Come and sit over here, Mike. We've got all the tables sorted out.'

As I sat down, one of the WRAFs named Christine whom I had known for a little while, sat next to me. She put her arm around my shoulder, and whispered in a seductive voice into my ear, 'Do you mind if I look after you for the whole evening, Mike?'

As I was in a high state of excitement, I replied. 'No my darling, you look after me for as long as you like.' With that, I gave her a little peck on the cheek. I don't know what perfume she had on, but she smelt absolutely fabulous. Christine was a tall, long-haired brunette. She was of Irish descent, and worked next door in Flight Ops. All the time I had known her she had been very amiable towards me. She had a lovely oval-shaped face, and a beautiful figure that was admired by many of the lads in the camp. I had fancied her for a long time myself, but had not made any advances towards her, because I was afraid that I would have the embarrassment of being turned down, particularly, due to my being a National Serviceman with little money, and her being a regular, earning a lot more than I. Many an erk had made it known that they would have liked to make a date with her. But no one, as far as I know, had gone out with her. There was some talk that she might be an officer's girl, or that she may be a lesbian. But no one was certain. She was a girl who kept everyone guessing. A real mystery girl.

That evening was an evening that stood out above all booze-ups. I drank cider, Tiger beer and different drinks of all descriptions. I ended the evening not drunk, but a very happy fellow. I don't know how much I drank, but it must have been a hell of a lot.

Come the end of the party Christine helped me down the steps from the Chalet Club and led me towards the Pagar, and the beach.

'Come on, Mike. Are you as bad as you make out you are?' she asked, as we walked across the grass alone.

'Let's put it this way. Christine my love,' I started. 'I've had a skinful. I still know what I'm doing. But,' I added, 'I'm happy with it. You know what I mean.'

She nodded and laughed, as we walked arm in arm together, feeling the warm night air on our faces.

'I'll tell you something else, my gorgeous. This is not the way to get me back to my billet,' I said laughing, feeling as lighthearted as could be.

'Like I said, Mike. I'm here to look after you on your last night, and it's going to be one of best nights you'll ever remember, my darling,' said Christine.

With that she leant over towards me and gave me a peck on the cheek. 'You're a bit of an odd one, Mike Baker. I've wanted to get you alone for ages.'

'Well, I do my own thing, you know,' I said as I returned the kiss.

We walked across the Pagar, towards some benches that were situated on the edge of the beach. As we got close to the seats, Christine whispered, 'Not here, Mike. Let's go over amongst those trees and bushes.'

We went in amongst the bushes, so that no one could see us from the camp area. But the view over the beach and the bay was wonderful, with the moon glowing bright and reflecting on the sea, the masts and yachts swaying in the slight swell of the sea. Every now and then you would see phosphorus flashing in the water. It was a very warm and very romantic setting.

Christine sat down on the grass, pulling me down towards her, making sure that our lips met. 'Mike, you just don't know how I've dreamed of having you alone, all to myself. Now that I have you, and you're going home tomorrow, I want to make this a night that both of us will always remember.'

I lay down on the grass beside her, and quietly whispered, 'I didn't know you felt like this towards me. Why in the name of hell, didn't you say something to me before?'

I kissed her very tenderly on the lips, and as I put my arms around her I could feel a breast pushing up against me.

We lay in amongst the bushes at the side of the Pagar, for some time. We made passionate love, which was, without doubt, one of the best evenings I had spent with a woman. Christine certainly made it a night that I shall never forget. It was sheer bliss and there's one thing that was certain – she was no lesbian.

It must have been around two or three o'clock in the morning that I got back to my billet, after taking Christine back to hers. Usually,

WRAFs had to be in by a certain time. But, if for any good reason they had wanted to stay out late at night they were issued with a pass. I must have just been dozing off to sleep, at around 03.30 or 04.00 hours when a lot of shouting, cursing and laughter woke me up.

'What the bloody hell's going on?' I shouted out from my pit.

Terry came running in from the veranda. 'Come on out Mike, Steve and Bob have just come back from their all-day rave up.'

'So what of it,' I came back at him.

'Come on Mike. Get up. It's the biggest laugh yet,' he said laughing.

I got up, and went out onto the veranda, to find Steve and Bob in a very enraged mood, to say the least.

'What's up with you two?' I said to Steve.

'Don't you f**** start,' he shouted rudely at me, in his Yorkshire accent.

I got a little angry myself when Steve turned on me for no apparent reason. 'Hey! Hey! I said. 'What's all this about? I've only just gone off to sleep. The next thing you come in at this time of night, wake us all up with all this aggro!' I shouted back. 'Now calm down. What's the problem?'

'No! I'm not telling you, because, if I did, you'd only start laughing, the same as the rest are,' shouted Bob indignantly.

With that, some of the lads around started to laugh out more loudly than ever.

'I wish one of you bastards would let me in on the joke,' I asked out loud 'so that I can see the funny side of it as well.' I was by now beginning to come out of my sleepy daze.

Len, one of the other erks in the billet, came up to me, put his arm around my shoulder, partly to support himself more than anything, and, laughing so much that tears were streaming down his cheeks. 'Haven't you heard what happened to them. Mike?' Len started to laugh uncontrollably. He started to tell me, in between his bursts of laughter.

After Steve and Bob had picked up their hired car from Changi village, they drove into Singapore City. During the morning, they picked up two women in a café. From all accounts the two women were absolutely fabulously good-looking. They took them with them wherever they went. They went here and there: Tiger Balm Gardens, Orchard Road and the Odeon cinema for the afternoon Matinée, and

Capital Cinema in the evening. They went to every place they could think of before they were due to go back to Blighty. They spent their money like there was no tomorrow. Both were determined to have a good time. They did everything that they wanted.

Come the evening, after going to another restaurant, it was decided that it had been a wonderful day and it was time to finish it off with the girls. Have a kiss and a cuddle, then take them home.

Steve, who was driving the car, had his girl seated in the passenger seat beside him, and Bob was in the back with his girl. All through the day, since they had picked up the girls, they had been stealing little kisses, etc.

They drove to a little spot off the road and out of town, after which, Steve started to snog with his girl in the front seat, whilst Bob did the same on the back seat with his girl.

From all accounts, they were getting really passionate towards the girls. They fondled their little breasts, until all of them couldn't stand it any longer and the girls opened their legs for the lads to put their hands up them.

Did they get a surprise when they caught hold of a nice pair of balls!

From what was told after they had come back to camp. They completely lost control. They bundled the two 'girls' out of the car and gave them something they didn't expect – that was a bloody good hiding. I don't expect the girls were a pretty sight, after they had finished with them. They came back to camp completely broke, and very angry gentlemen indeed. They had enjoyed themselves wonderfully; they had spent their money, not only on themselves but on the 'girls' as well, especially, as they had both thought that they were on to a good thing. How disappointed they must have been when they found out that the two girls were in fact men . . .

After I heard the story I couldn't help but laugh at their unfortunate experience. I really could see the funny side of the story. The more Steve and Bob got angry in the billet, the more everyone laughed, and so they got even more enraged. Steve, especially, was absolutely fuming.

Because of the loud laughter in the billet, the noise gradually woke other parts of the billet up as well. Then came shouts from other billets nearby for us to keep quiet. But as soon as those billets were told of what had happened one could hear chuckles all around the camp. The RAF police were called to get some semblance of order, but as soon as they heard the story even they started to see the funny side of things and joined in the laughter.

In the end, come the morning, everyone, regardless of rank, had heard what had happened, and was laughing. It's the only time that I saw the whole camp going around its business with a kind of smirk on its face, and that included the WRAFs.

It was also my last day before I left RAF Changi for the very last time. I was due to take off at midnight, which I was not looking forward to. However, after sending my luggage to the flight movement hangar I decided to spend a little time in Changi village, and also to go and see some of my friends who were in the married quarters. I also spent some time in the swimming pool, where I had not been far from, whilst spending a wonderful few hours with Christine in the early hours that same morning. I had also made arrangements to meet Christine again after dark, which I must confess, was more emotional than I had anticipated.

Finally, the time came for me to report to Air Movements so I could board the Comet 4C that was to take me home. As I boarded the aircraft it was approx. 23.30 hours. At the top of the steps I stopped and looked around the camp for the very last time. I waved to those few friends that were on the top of the bank to see me off and quietly said goodbye to the place I had come to love so much, and which I didn't want to leave. I had memories that would never, never be forgotten.

At exactly midnight the Comet started to roll along the runway, gathering speed, eventually lifting off the ground to set a course for Gan Island, which was a four hour-flight to the middle of the Indian Ocean. We landed there at 02.30 hours local time. After re-fuelling, which took about one and half hours, the aircraft set off for Khormaksar in Aden, to refuel once again. All the hops appeared to take around four hours, landing at 06.00 hours local time. From Aden, the route took us over the African continent, making for El Adem in Libya.

The route to El Adem was not a direct flight because of diplomatic problems with Egypt. The plane was not allowed to fly into Egyptian air space, so we took a westerly route over Ethiopia, and then northerly, over Sudan and then to El Adem in Libya, arriving in the middle of nowhere at approximately midday.

The runway at El Adem was a straightforward cross to allow aircraft to land into the wind from whatever direction the wind was coming. As we approached the airfield, at about ten thousand feet, and descending, the first thing that grabbed my attention at El Adem was the bleak situation of the airfield. It was in the middle of the desert, with nothing around it for miles and miles. Not a thing could be seen but desert. As the aircraft began to circle the airfield to land, I noticed right in the middle of the airfield where the two runways crossed each other, there appeared to be a great swath of sand across the runway. The other thing which was standing out from the golden desert was a small dot of blue. It stood out like a sore thumb and turned out to be the only form of relaxation that the staff at El Adem had. That was the swimming pool.

After re-fuelling, we set off for RAF Lyneham. The ETA for Lyneham was 19.00 hours local time. After a flight of some twenty odd hours, and with the time jumps, we had come some ten thousand kilometres, to be home in England for what one could say, was in time for tea the same day.

On board the Comet 4C were not only RAF personnel, but also sailors, and army personnel as well. You must remember that I had the chance to take the last troopship a few months earlier. Now all military staff were flown by the Royal Air Force to whatever destination. Also amongst the passengers were a lot of Gurkha soldiers. The Gurkhas were a distinguished lot of soldiers, rather on the small side, but very tough. All the military had the greatest respect for them. They were renowned for their jungle fighting and there are a lot of soldiers who were glad that they were on the Allied side, and not that of the Japanese.

I was sitting across the seat from one group of them. I got talking to them, and finally the subject came up of where they were going, once in Blighty.

'We're going to guard the Queen,' said one, in a very, very proud voice.

I replied to the effect, 'Where, Buckingham Palace?'

'Yes! Buckingham Palace and Windsor Castle,' one of them answered.

God, they were a proud bunch of lads. It was as if they had been given their life's ambition. There is no doubt, while they were guarding the Queen, Her Majesty would have been in the safest of hands. They would have put their own lives before her. Not that I'm saying that the English military would not have given their lives either, but the Gurkhas were a proud race of chaps.

The aircraft landed in the most obnoxious weather. It was grey, dark, and raining. I remember as the aircraft came over the main road to touch down. A motor cyclist was driving along the road. He was dressed in a black leather waterproof jacket, and leggings to match. With his crash helmet and goggles on he looked absolutely shrammed with the cold. What a welcome home, I thought. Back to dear old Blighty and the cold weather.

As we all got off the plane to go to the Customs hall I happened to look behind me. Perhaps, it was to take a final look at the Comet, I don't really know. But as I looked, I saw a few of the Gurkhas walking away from the plane. All they had on were their summer-wear uniforms, and wearing on top of that, a very thin Pak-a-Mac. They looked absolutely frozen. I know that they are a hardy race, but my heart went out to them. I felt like taking off the overcoat that had been made for me, by Thia Chin Tailors in Changi village, and handing it to one of them, so at least one was getting the benefit of a warm coat. The last I saw of them was them entering the Customs hall.

As we ourselves entered the Customs hall we were ushered past some low tables. Behind the tables were the Customs Officers. We were asked by HM Customs Officers what we had brought back from abroad. I didn't have much with me, as most of my personal belongings and presents had been packed away in my deep sea chest. The chest, which I packed, had been sent on by cargo plane from Singapore, a couple of months earlier. I was hoping that it would be home by the time I arrived.

After going through the Customs hall, all the passengers were taken off by whatever means had been arranged for them. In my case, I was issued with a railway pass, and taken by coach to Swindon railway station. I caught the train to Bristol, and from there went by taxi to my home.

I had not written and told my parents when I was likely to come home, but my last letter had said that it was to be the last one, and that I wasn't sure when I would be arriving home. The taxi took me to the address I had given. I paid the driver, turned around to see the house that I hadn't seen for nearly two years. I was back home and was about to see my parents again.

There was a large tree growing opposite the front door which stopped the street light illuminating the front door so anyone who was by the front door would be in the shadows, and not seen very well. I came to the front door and rang the door bell. Since I had been in a hot climate for a longish time I had become a very dark tanned person. I stood back in the dark shadows of the tree. The door opened, and a voice said. 'Yes? Can I help you?' It was my aunt, my mother'a sister.

'Is this where Mrs Baker lives?' I asked.

'Yes,' came the reply. My aunt had not recognised my voice. Had that changed as well?

'Would it be possible to see her, please?'

With that my aunt went back indoors. 'There's some chap outside wants to see you,' I heard my aunt say to my mother.

'Who is it?' I heard my mother enquire.

'I don't know who it is,' my aunt replied.

The door opened again. There stood my mother. She looked into the darkness, but still couldn't see who it was. 'Yes?' my mother enquired again.

'Mrs Baker?' I asked.

'Yes!' my mother confirmed. 'What can I do for you?' she enquired, just the same as her sister had only a few minutes earlier. 'Who are you?' she enquired of me. She still could not see who stood in the dark.

'Don't you know me?' I asked, not moving. 'Aren't you going to welcome your son home then?' I said as I took one step forward into the light of the hallway light.

My mother leapt forward, wrapping her arms around her son.

I was indeed home.

Epilogue

Singapore and Changi Revisited

RECENTLY, (JANUARY 1992 AND 1993) I had the good fortune to visit my old base at Changi in Singapore with my wife – a dream that I never thought would come true. To those many of thousands of ex-RAF personnel who were ever posted to Changi and have often wondered what the old place is like now, I would like to give my description below of the changes to Singapore, and Changi itself, hoping that it brings back some glorious memories.

Singapore has changed quite considerably but the old RAF Changi has not. There were quite a few surprises there when I revisited, and yet there were many changes that I thought would have happened, which had not. For instance, Changi village had changed with more up to date houses and shops, but Changi Point is the same now as it was more than thirty years ago. The old transit block in the village that was completely surrounded by trees has now been cleared and is in the open and has been given to the Red Cross. When I saw it, it was in a rather dilapitated state and was being renovated by prisoners from Changi Jail.

Changi Jail hasn't altered as such. But where I use to see it clear from the road to the walls – not anymore – there is a great big security fence completely surrounding it, right up to the main road (Main Road as we remember it, is another alteration). The Old Changi Road, or Upper Changi Road. has not altered, except it is not the main road to the city anymore. The crossroads at the corner of the jail, the one that used to take one to HMS *Terror* (Navy Dock and Loyang) and down to Changi Beach at the back of 205 squadron, on the far side of the airfield – well, that is a four-lane main road to Singapore

City, and is commonly known as an expressway. It's one of the main highways to the new Singapore Changi Airport, the new airport terminal buildings being situated more or less over where the Shackletons of 205 squadron and the Bristol freighters of RAAF or RNZAF used to be. Of course, the land has been reclaimed, and goes out a lot further.

Singapore Island itself has now been completely built on. There is hardly any space left, and places that used to be little villages (Kampongs) are now built up areas, with modern flats, and are merging into one another. As they can't go any further out they have started to build up. In fact, they had started to do that whilst I was out there in the 1960s. They say that more than ninety per cent of the population are now living in high-rise flats

The city, and the country, was once commonly accepted as the gutter of Malaya. It certainly isn't that now. I have never been in such a clean country in all my life. Metaphorically speaking, you could eat off the pavements there. Chewing gum is banned from being brought into the country. You are not allowed to drop any litter whatsoever, or spit. Failing to adhere to these laws means an instant fine of nine hundred dollars (three hundred pounds approximately). Plus if you are caught drug dealing the penalty is death. With no ifs or buts. They really are very strict. To remind everyone, every other lamp-post or so, has a sign on it reminding the people of the consequences for dropping litter. At times I wish they would introduce laws of this severity in the UK.

It's so safe in Singapore that a woman could go out on her own to any place she wished and be as safe as could be. It really is a place where one feels at ease, no matter what time of day, or night, it is.

Can you imagine Singapore River, Anderson Bridge, with king-fishers, and people fishing there? Believe me, I saw both. A blue kingfisher perched on a branch by the Anderson Bridge, with people fishing on the river bank, down on Queen Elizabeth Walk. In fact I watched a local fisherman land quite a sizeable fish at Queen Elizabeth Walk.

There were only a few places that I could remember when I first arrived, until I got my bearings again. I had a job to find some of my old haunts, but you will be pleased to know that the old Britannia Club is still there, opposite the Raffles. Of course, it isn't known as the Britannia Club now, although it still belongs to the military. (Singapore A F SNCOs Club)

There are one or two places that have unfortunately gone. One is Change Alley by Robinsons Square, and Fullerton Buildings. Change Alley is there, but across the road in Cliffords Pier and it's not quite Change Alley as we knew it, just a row of bizarre shops, with the old atmosphere just not in evidence. Other places that have gone are the Worlds (Happy, Old and New) Another place that was destroyed, but fortunately, has now been put back as it was is Bugis Street. In the tourist brochures, it is stated that Bugis Street is just like its notorious past, with drinking bars, etc, except that its notoriety has been cleaned up. (No girls!) Don't you believe it!

I found that the people are still very friendly, courteous and extremely smart. They have become very Westernised. You don't see the traditional clothes like it used to be. When I was out there thirty odd years ago one would see a lot of women wearing *Chiong Foo's* (trouser suits) or *Cheong Sams* (dresses) – not any more. They all wear Western-type clothing. The girls wearing a lot of designer clothing. You may see one or two Malayan (Moslem) type dresses, or Saris from the Indian women, but then you see that anywhere in the world. (Indian Saris) As for the men? Well, they are completely Westernised, apart from Chinatown, where you might see an occasional traditional dress. This was one of the things that surprised me – was the disappearance of traditional dress.

Another thing that has more or less gone are the trishaws (tricycles). They have them, but just for tourism. You can be walking around town, and have them come to you asking if you want a ride. There must be about a couple of hundred of them or so. But you only find them in the city centre. I certainly wouldn't like to be riding in one of them nowadays, with the traffic there. The roads used to be mad enough before, but now it's even worse than ever. All main roads are basically dual carriageways or one-way systems. For instance, Bras Basah Road, the road that goes from the Britannia Club up to the Capital cinema (which is still there) used to be two-way traffic. Not anymore; it is a five-lane road coming down from Orchard Road (Capital cinema) and goes on past the Brit Club onto Nicoll Highway (the road where the Merdeka Bridge is situated). And it is busy, it's more like a race track. Even Orchard Road has five lanes and one-way flow of traffic, which comes down towards the city. Now Nicoll Highway, if you remember, used to be the Coastal Road that led onto East Coast Road, past the old Kallang airfield. Not anymore, the land has been reclaimed, and goes a long way out to sea. As for the old Kallang airfield itself, that has become the main National Sports Stadium and recreation area, and very nice it is too.

Now let me tell you about the biggest change in Singapore that I saw. This was the new underground railway, or MRT (Mass Rapid Transit) as they call it. I haven't seen many underground railways, but this from what I have been told by other people who have had that experience, is without doubt the most clean, safe and the cheapest underground one could use, throughout the world. I can well believe this. All tickets are bought from a machine, and rolling stock is completely automated. The maximum cost is one dollar seventy (approximately sixty pence) for the furthest distance (the length of the island). The platforms are like marble, and so clean and reflective you could easily look down into it and comb your hair. When standing at the edge of the platform it is impossible to be pushed down, or to commit suicide there. The full length of the edge of the platform is completely lined with a glass and metal screening, with sliding doors at regular intervals. When a train pulls onto the platform the trains stop at a predetermined spot. Both the train doors and the platform doors slide open simultaneously (just like lift doors) to allow passengers on and off. When the train is due to move off a bell or hooter sounds. Then the doors close and the train moves off, leaving the platform doors still closed. The trains themselves come and go every few minutes. They are the same as the rest of the city, as clean as a whistle.

One place that has changed for the better is what was known as Blakang Mati Island. This is where the big guns were situated (pointing the wrong way out to sea). The island has now become a leisure island. Now known under the name of Sentosa Island (Island of Tranquillity). To get there, you go by either ferry, or cable car. I went over by cable car; and what a fantastic ride that was. You go from Mount Fabar across to the island at a height between three to five hundred feet. The view you get is really out of this world. You can see the whole of the Singapore City skyline, and more. The only black spot of the trip, if you can call it that, is as you go over the edge of Keppel Docks. Even then, the docks seem to go on for ever and ever. They really are sprawling. Once you are over on the island, you pay a fee of seven dollars fifty. Then you can go anywhere on the island by Monorail. Other places which are included as part of the price are Fort Silosa (where the big guns are) museums, nature walks, coralarium, etc. There were one or two places you had to pay to go in, but not many.

At the top of the island there was a big arena. One could sit down at any time during the day or the evening, and watch a musical and dancing fountain. During the evening, the fountains were floodlit, and gave out different colours in time with the music. The size of the fountains has to be seen to be believed. The whole area covers something in the range of about two hundred feet and went back about a hundred feet, with two massive circles at the edge of the arena, with the whole complex shaped in a crescent. Singapore has made a real leisure centre and enjoyable island of it. We shall certainly want to go there again.

We also went to Haw Par Villas (Tiger Balm Gardens) Tiger Balm is exactly the same as it always was – very colourful, and full of Chinese mythology. The difference that I saw, was that it has become very soft in its approach. If you remember, there were one or two pieces that were rather gruesome, and full of blood and guts. (Old Chinese tortures as an example). Today, the emphasis is on family enjoyment, which I think is only right. Another thing that has changed is that we never used to pay to enter. Today you do. Mind you, I'm not complaining, because it was still inexpensive.

Now to the important part of my visit to Singapore, and that, of course was to see our old camp at Changi. We got up in the morning, and caught the MRT to the nearest station to Changi. From there we got a taxi and asked for Changi village via Changi Jail. It wasn't until we approached Changi Jail that I realised where we were. As I said earlier, the area had changed out of all recognition. When the taxi turned right (I now realise where we were heading, but I didn't at the time), I was completely lost. I still didn't realise where I was, until the taxi stopped in Changi village, because Telok Pekot Road was now a main crossroad with lights. It led to the new Singapore Changi airport terminals. My wife and I got out. It took me a minute or so to get my bearings until I realised that we were actually in Changi village. I don't mind admitting, it really was a very nostalgic and emotional day for me, I had a lump in my throat quite often during my tour of old RAF Changi. I could see that we had got out at the top of the village, not far from the new five-star hotel Meridian Changi Hotel. The hotel was roughly opposite the old transit block. We had only to go around

the corner to get to the Nuffield swimming pool, which I will come
to later on. It felt ever so strange to be back after all those years. After
I had got my bearings, we walked down through the village. There
weren't as many people there to what I was used to seeing. Just the
odd villager or two, and a few   Singapore military personnel.
Admittedly, we were there a little early, around ten a.m. Anyway, we
walked down the left-hand side of the road looking at the different
shops that were there.

Eventually, we stopped at one shop that stood just round the corner
from where I use to sit and have coffee and jam butties. Well, the alley
that used to be behind Fred's Alley Café is now a large wide shopping
precinct that goes back almost to the river.

While my wife was in a shop buying some presents, I sat outside
with the shop owner and talked about old times. He stated that in
1960-2 he was a boy of only about seven years of age, but remembered some of those days. He told me quite a few things of interest –
of what was still here and what was gone. One of the things I enquired
was the whereabouts of Mary Tan OBE. The shopowner stated that
she had died quite a while back. I wasn't surprised to hear this news,
as she had been in her late forties whilst I was out there.

He did say that business was nowhere near like it used to be, especially since the RAF left. They get a few tourists, but not many. Very
occasionally they might see one, or two old ex-RAF merchants (like
myself) there. Most of the tourists were Japanese and a few Australians,
and even then, not many visited Changi village because the village was
slightly off the beaten track from the Singapore Airport terminals and
Singapore City. I must have talked to him for at least an hour. We
bought the presents after a little bartering, and went on our way.

I had one of my biggest surprises when we got to the end of the
village. There on the corner of Telok Pekot Road was George's
Camera shop. Obviously I had to go in, and see what it was like now.
Outside the shop was almost the same placard with the 'no shit prices'
displayed. I went inside to find that the son was still running the
business. The old man had died a few years earlier. I was told to call
the son George as well. As soon as I mentioned that I had been out
here more than thirty years ago out came all the old photos of years
ago. His shop was renowned around the village, as a museum for
photos. George spoke the best English I had heard while I was out
there this time – not only in Changi village, but in the whole of

Singapore. I must have been in his shop for at least an hour and a half, if not more, talking about old times. He acted as if he had met an old personal friend. When I eventually said that I had to make a move so that I could show my wife around the old camp, he gave me the impression he didn't want me to go.

We walked on up the old Changi Road towards Tangmere Road and towards where the old Com-cen Changi was. We turned left into Churchdown Road, the road that went round to the Com-cen, via the mosque. We got to the mosque, which hadn't changed one iota, only to have to turn back again due to the road being demolished, and fenced off. A couple of Muslims who were on their way to prayers asked if they could help us. I explained what I was doing, looking up my old base, after thirty odd years. They informed me that the road had to be demolished because the aircraft were now that much bigger, and the new wing-span would have caught the edge of the bank. We then walked back, and around to the barrack square, only to find the only building in the camp that I worked in (block 106) had been demolished. Also the married families' club had been pulled down. Below the bank at Churchdown Road the original runway had been made so long, that it now ran right behind Changi Jail, and Changi Hill was no longer there. It had been completely flattened to accommodate the old runway extension. An additional runway is situated behind the new terminal buildings on reclaimed land, which goes out to sea at least half a mile further than we used to know. Changi Beach as we knew it is still there, but is further out from its original position.

From there we proceeded towards Tangmere Road and on up towards block 144. The road and the guardhouse were still there. It wasn't being used as such, and looked a little bit weathered. Tangmere Road itself was the same, and as we walked up it it was just as if time had stood still. As we turned left into Old Sarum Road towards block 144, I noticed that where the WOs and the Fire Brigade were billeted, although the buildings themselves were still there, and in good condition, it was all fenced off. We came to the corner to go into Martlesham Road, towards block 144. The road here too was fenced off, and a gate right across the road was locked. The same for the road towards the old Sergeants' Mess, except that the gate towards it was open. We walked through towards the Sergeants' Mess and were met by an airman of the Republic of Singapore Air Force. He phoned up somewhere to explain that I had a letter of authority to visit the camp.

For some reason or other, we didn't get very far with them, but they did allow us to walk on down the road and we were escorted, which was fair enough. While we were at the end of Old Sarum Road, I noticed that the old entrance to the air maintenance area was now fenced off and the old Changi Road as well so that no one could get from, or to the airfield, or, on towards Changi Jail. Moreover, the old aircraft parking area had some buildings in the middle of it.

From there we walked back to Tangmere Road and down towards where the Astra Cinema stood (which had, incidentally, gone). The fencing ran all the way down the left hand side of the road so that you couldn't get to the old Malcolm Club, or the old WRAFs' billet. When we got to the bottom of Tangmere Road I noticed that the old Airmen's Mess was still an Airmen's Mess. We walked round the corner and back towards block 144. Here was another change. Where there used to be the postbox on the corner of Martlesham Road it was a guardhouse.

As we approached it one of the guards walked up to us and said, 'We have been expecting you. Have you come to see the murals?' I stated that I had, and had come to see my old billet. Once again, we were escorted to the murals by what seemed a very young soldier (hard to believe I was once his age out there). Anyway, we were escorted not along Martlesham Road, but around the back of the old NAAFI, which was also a Mess now.

We were taken to block 151 where the murals were. You will remember the murals were in a rather dilapidated state. Not now – four paintings have been completely renovated by the original artist, Stanley Warren. The fifth painting is in the process of being redone. Unfortunately, we heard later that this fifth painting would not be completed due to the fact that Mr Warren had died. Thirty-odd years ago, the room was just an empty room but now, it has been made into a proper chapel. My wife asked where the flowers came from. The soldier stated that they were changed every day, and paid for by the Singapore Tourist Board. The thing that came to my mind was the myth about the murals coming back to their original state. I never believed that it would be so. But here they were as the legend had foretold, back to their original condition, except one.

We came out of block 151 and I pointed out to my wife and our young escort that the billet across the way was my old billet. We walked up towards it. Unfortunately, it had been padlocked, so I was unable to enter. It was at this particular time, and I don't know why, but my emotions came over me, and I shed a few tears. On thinking back, it was possibly when I noticed the bar across the veranda, which was just outside my room, was still missing after thirty odd years.

From there we went on down Cranwell Road. That is the main road on towards Temple Hill and HQFEAF. The first place we passed was the old MT Section and it still is an MT Section. We walked on towards the junction for Temple Hill. At this junction was another gate with a guardhouse, again all fenced off. I was beginning to wonder, why all this security? We then came to the new museum. The museums are on the crest of the hill. What used to be Trinity Church and Hall, and the Roman Catholic Church. Behind the museums is a static display of different aircraft that the Republic of Singapore Air Force are using, or have used. My wife and I were wondering whether to go in or not, but I decided in the end that since we had come this far, and it was now getting rather hot – as it was about two or three in the afternoon – we might as well go in.

Whilst we were looking at the exhibits on the history of the Singapore Air Force and the mementos they had, an officer came up to us and asked if he could help. I replied that everything was alright, and that I was here just visiting my old camp after approximately thirty years. We were ushered into an ante-room, and given a cool drink, which I must confess couldn't have come at a better time for both my wife and me. It really was a hot day outside, and we were very dry.

I showed him an old book. (It was the original book that was given to me, on my initial walk-about the camp when I first arrived, back in 1960.) I was using it to help me around the camp, and also to help me see the differences. He asked if I would donate the book to the museum, as they had very few mementos of pre-Singapore Air Force days (1971). I asked if they had a photo-copier, to which he replied that they had. I let him have the book to photocopy. Whilst this was being done, I talked about the old days, and what the camp was like in my days. It appears that they have very little in the way of artefacts in the museum as regards the RAF days. They were very interested in my reminiscences. By now there was an additional officer with us. I suppose we were in the museum for about one and a half hours all told. One thing that I did ask was about the fencing around the camp. The answer came as quite a surprise. The Changi camp is now split into three sections. One is the Army, another was for the commandos, or infantry (I don't know what the difference is) and the third was the Air Force. So now I could understand that all the fencing around the camp waso keep the different sections apart. (It's a wonder they never had the Navy there as well). We were treated very well. I must admit it was very nice talking to them about the old camp as I knew it. What I liked most was that they listened and were genuinely interested.

From there we walked on, after refusing, although with great appreciation, a lift back to the hotel in Singapore City. We walked down the road to the crossroads where the Church of England church was situated. As expected, it was still there. Now the road that was known as Farnborough Road (now known as Loyang Avenue) which led back to the village, via the playing fields at the back of the school, has become a main road from the village back to Singapore City. It is part of the crossroads with the village high street, and Telok Pekot Road. The school itself is no longer there, and has become a maintenance area. We walked up over towards the hospital. Glory be, the hospital was still there and it is still known as Changi Hospital. We walked past there, and down towards the swimming pool, by the Pagar. The Pagar is still there, and the NAAFI (Chalet Club) that stood at the top of the Pagar Steps was still there except that it is no longer the NAAFI but part of the hospital complex. The other thing was that they had allowed the trees to grow a lot taller. The biggest surprise of all, however was the swimming pool.

There is just no comparison with bygone days. It has now become a private club, and is a full Olympic-sized swimming pool with all the facilities to go with it. The steps down to the entrance were still there, and that was the only thing that had not changed.

From there we went onto see Changi Point, etc, and back into the village (more or less from where we started). The village has changed, but not to the extent that I had imagined it would have. Yes, there are now pavements. Yes, the shops are no longer hovels but shops with proper flats above. The character, and the atmosphere seem to be still there, as are the trees lining the village. All in all, I thought the day was magnificent. I know my wife enjoyed herself, because she had seen all the places that I had spoken to her about in the past.

There is some talk of Changi becoming a holiday resort for tourism, so you never know. If the Singapore Tourist Board advertise Changi as a holiday resort in Britain a few more ex-erks may try to return.

As regards the holiday in Singapore itself, well, I don't think I would like to live there now. Whereas, before our visit, I always said that I would, the reason I have changed my mind is that, although the place still holds that special magic for me, there just isn't the room there now – everything appears rather crowded. Not that it appears overcrowded as regards people. It's no different now than it was then. No! what I am talking about is the amount of buildings that have sprung up. There's hardly any countryside there now, although the area still appears to be as green as ever, it has all been built up. Singapore itself – I loved it. There are some very good improvements, but at the same time, due to progress, some of the places involving nostalgia have gone. Overall, I think Singapore is better now than it was around three decades ago. The reasons are that it is MUCH, MUCH CLEANER, SAFER, and yet THE PEOPLE ARE STILL THE SAME. Also it *still has that atmosphere*. So much so, my wife wants to go there again but not to wait as long as I did.